LIVING THE
LIFE
—OF—
PROVERBS

Also by Kevin M. Thomas:

Why Daughters Need Their Dads
The Happiest Women
Chinese Spiritual Thoughts
The Great Path
Wisdom and Virtue
The Tao Te Ching De-Coded

LIVING THE
LIFE
—OF—
PROVERBS

*The Biblical Blueprint
for True Happiness*

KEVIN M. THOMAS

LIVING THE LIFE OF PROVERBS

The Biblical Blueprint for True Happiness

KETNA Publishing
P.O. Box 90861 Burton, MI 48509
© 2022 by Kevin M. Thomas

For more information, address to KETNA Publishing
P.O. Box 90861, Burton, MI 48509
First KETNA Printing Edition 2022

Book Cover Designer: TopHills
Cover Design by: 99Designs
Book Interior and E-book Design by: Amit Dey | amitdey2528@gmail.com
Proofreading by Kelly Bixler and Judy Seitz of www.thewriteproofreader.com

Printed in the USA

Library of Congress Control Number: 2022915270

ISBN: 978-1-948265-02-7(soft cover)
ISBN 978-1-948265-03-4 (hard cover)
ISBN 978-1-948265-04-1 (e-book)

Dedication

First, this book is dedicated to God. He has given me grace, mercy, forgiveness, discernment, and wisdom. He has given me miracles and comfort during tough times. He walked with me, and he carried me. He has allowed me to share his love, peace, compassion, and kindness so others will seek his grace and love. Second, it is dedicated to you the reader, may you always be blessed on your spiritual path.

Acknowledgments

I want to thank my parents, June and Grover, now resting in the arms of Jesus. I put them through some tough times, and they always responded with unconditional love. I look forward to seeing them again.

To those genuinely supportive souls who stand by me and continue to do so, I thank you, and you know who you are.

Table of Contents

What Makes
This Book Special

Living the Life of Proverbs is a unique look at one of the most popular books in the Bible. All thirty-one chapters of Proverbs are summarized and alternated in groups for easy understanding. Over 120 personal character traits are then put into fourteen categories to help people understand the various areas of life to work on in order to become not only a better Christian but also a growing person.

You will find guidance in the following areas: business, character, communication, demeanor, discipline, generosity, forgiveness, justice, loyalty, parenting, sex, teaching, wisdom, and worshipping God.

Introduction

Proverbs are often described as short sayings of God's wisdom, offering practical instructions on how we can live and the importance of the fear of the Lord. The Hebrew word translated as *proverb* can also be translated as *oracle* (i.e., a person through whom God is speaking), *taunt* (i.e., remarks made to provoke further action), and *parable* (i.e., a simple story used to illustrate a moral or spiritual lesson). Proverbs were written primarily for instruction or in the form of commands with the desired action being quite clear. The book of Proverbs often uses metaphors, general observations, character traits, and consequences to guide those reading to make wise choices to shape their lives as members of the human community and God's community. Proverbs instructs the simpleminded to the most discerning of the wise. It guides the young and the old to avoid folly and pitfalls to create a better person, a happier family, and a greater community and multiplies the fruit of the Spirit in serving God. These words in Proverbs are the tree of life to help avoid pitfalls such as anger, violence, fighting, drunkenness, gluttony, arrogance, envy, and greed, and instead to focus on traits to enhance one's life: honesty, integrity, kindness, humility, patience, self-control, good temper, generosity, forgiveness, hard work, joy, and good cheer. It also helps to establish attitudes and actions that will influence proper choices and actions. They help people ultimately choose the way of wisdom that leads to life. Finally, obedience, fear and reverence for the Lord, and trust and commitment to the Lord lead to ultimate success for someone following the Lord. The book of Proverbs was created sometime between 715 and 686 BC in the tenth century during a time of spiritual renewal. Solomon, son of David, King of Israel, and the primary author, provided over 3,000 proverbs in his lifetime, 915 in the book of Proverbs alone. And while he likely produced most of it, he was not the sole author, as the "circle of wise men" also contributed, and it was "copied by the men of Hezekiah king of Judah." Aramaic spellings also may point to a non-Israelite background for some parts.

SECTION ONE

LIVING PROVERBS PASSAGES:

Chapters 1 through 31

CHAPTER 1

Things to Seek, Be, or Do

Chapter 1 lays the foundation for all 31 chapters for young men and all people. It begins by emphasizing trust and reverence for God. It indicates the importance of exploring all nuggets of truth for the depth of meaning and understanding. It mentions honoring one's mother and father, and that all of these things are the foundation and beginning of wisdom. Here, the word *wisdom* appears several times, and the wise are advised to become even more insightful until their very beings become filled with the spirit of wisdom. With this accumulating knowledge and understanding, they know how to act in every circumstance. They are wise enough to stay away from evil men and share with others until even the simpleminded become wise. Ultimately, Christians become leaders and servants of God who can positively react to the world by being fair, justified, and understanding.

Chapter 1
Key Points: Things to Seek, Be, or Do

1. Follow Proverbs to learn how to live and act in every circumstance.
2. Be understanding, just, and fair in everything you do.
3. Read God's words to become wise rather than remaining simpleminded.
4. You will find warnings about problems you may face.
5. If you are already wise, God's words help you become wiser.
6. Become a leader by finding the depth of meaning from the nuggets of truth.
7. Have trust and reverence for the Lord, which is the beginning of wisdom.
8. Listen to your mother and father, for it will bring you many honors.
9. Have and develop the spirit of wisdom.
10. Be like the bird that avoids the traps of life.
11. Listen to wisdom, which calls out to everyone for a hearing.
12. If you listen to wisdom, you will live in peace and safety and be unafraid.

CHAPTER 1

What God Wants Us to Avoid

Chapter 1 shows that rejecting God in any manner will lead to that person's demise. This rejection is recognized by many names: fools, scoffers, mockers, spurners, criminals, looters, and murderers. Specifically, these are the fools who refuse wise teaching. These are the criminals who set their self-inflicted traps when they murder or commit robbery. These are the scoffers of wisdom and facts. These are the spurners of counsel and reproof. These people have turned their backs on God, despising his advice, and therefore, eat bitter fruit. These people have closed their eyes to the facts and do not trust God. Their complacency destroys them. Therefore, their punishment will be severe because they do not answer the call. These mockers will become mocked, and terror, anguish, and distress will surround the spurners. But they will receive no answer because it is too late; they have turned away from God to death. They demand their way, so they face the full terrors of the path they have chosen, and the violence they put upon others will result in their own violent death.

Chapter 1
Key Points: Things to Avoid

1. Don't be a fool who refuses to be taught.
2. Don't join bad men who rob and kill and who offer you equal shares of loot.
3. Stay far away from men who lead a life of crime.
4. Avoid crime, murder, and violence.
5. Don't be like criminals who tend to set their own booby traps.
6. If you use violence and murder, you will meet a violent death.
7. Don't be a fool or scoffer of wisdom and facts.
8. Don't be one who refuses to answer the call.
9. Don't disregard the excellent counsel of wisdom and reproof, for doing so will end in trouble.
10. If you mock others, you will be mocked and laughed at when you are in trouble.
11. Don't be the spurner whose terror, anguish, and distress will surround them with no answer.
12. Don't be the spurner who searches anxiously, but because you mocked God, your cry for   help will not be answered because it comes too late.
13. Don't close your eyes to facts and, therefore, show no trust in God.
14. If you turn your back on God and spurn advice, you will eat bitter fruit.
15. Don't demand your way, for it shows the full terrors of your chosen path.
16. Don't turn away from God, for it results in death; your complacency will kill you.

CHAPTER 2

Things to Seek, Be, or Do

Chapter 2 emphasizes listening and focusing on every word of the Lord, learning right from wrong, embracing wisdom and truth, and following the steps of a godly person to stay on the right path, specifically young men who listen, develop wisdom and good sense, gain insight and discernment, and acquire a more in-depth knowledge of God. The Lord grants them good sense to shield and protect their path. Every word of God leads to more knowledge and understanding. They learn right from wrong and how to make the right decision every time. The wise realize that wisdom and truth are at the very center of the being, and they develop the sense to stay away from evil, which includes prostitutes. In the end, only good men enjoy life in full.

Chapter 2
Key Points: Things to Seek, Be, or Do

1. Listen and obey these instructions, and you will be given wisdom and good sense.
2. Search for better insight and discernment as you would gold; then wisdom will be given to you and even the knowledge of God himself.
3. Understand that when the Lord grants wisdom, his every word is a treasure of knowledge and understanding.
4. If you are godly, you will be given good sense to guard your path like a shield.
5. Obey, for God will show you how to know right from wrong and make the right decision *every* time.
6. Follow God's wisdom and truth, for it will permeate your inner being and give your life joy.
7. God will give you the sense to stay away from evil people.
8. Use wisdom to protect yourself from prostitutes.
9. Use wisdom to follow the steps of the godly that will help you stay on the right path.
10. You will enjoy life in full if you are a good person.

CHAPTER 2

What God Wants Us to Avoid

Chapter 2 discloses the doom that awaits those who actively seek and delight in destructive behavior. These are people who have turned from God and thoroughly enjoy sin, especially prostitution. Specifically, these people become crooked in their ways and follow dark and evil paths. These are the women who abandon their husbands to flaunt the laws of God and create houses of death and hell. God issues a warning: The men who enter these houses are doomed; they will never be the same again. Ultimately, all these evil men will lose their good things and be destroyed.

Chapter 2
Key Points: Things to Avoid

1. Don't be the evil man who turns from God.
2. Don't follow dark and evil paths.
3. Don't delight in wrongdoing.
4. Don't be one who is crooked and wrong and who thoroughly enjoys sin.
5. Avoid prostitutes who abandon their husbands and flaunt the laws of God.
6. Avoid the prostitute's house of death and hell.
7. Don't enter the prostitute's house or you'll never be the same and are doomed.
8. Don't be evil or you will lose the good things you have; they will be destroyed.

CHAPTER 3

Things to Seek, Be, or Do

Chapter 3 emphasizes turning one's back on evil and putting God first. When this happens, a person regains health and vitality. Trusting God directs a person's path and promotes good judgment and sense. He crowns their efforts with success. By following God's instruction, he creates truthful and kind people. He reminds them to give him the first part of their income and pay their debts, and he will overflow their barns and wine vats with food and drink. God tells his people to welcome punishment because it is proof of his love when he corrects them, as a father punishes a son he delights in and loves. God tells them they will be happier knowing right from wrong to make good decisions. He tells them that wisdom leads to a long useful life, riches, pleasures, honor, and peace. God says wisdom is the tree of life, and thrilled is the man who eats from it, adding that wisdom founded the Earth and established the universe. God tells his people to have two clear goals; to have wisdom and to have common sense, and that a combination of wisdom and common sense is a feather in their cap that (1) brings them living energy, (2) keeps them on the right trail, (3) keeps them safe, (4) lets them sleep with no fear, and (5) protects them from wicked plots and disasters. Simply said, the wise will be promoted to honor, the humble are helped, the upright become a blessing to others, and God gives his friendship to the Godly.

Chapter 3
Key Points: Things to Seek, Be, or Do

1. For a long and satisfying life, follow the instructions given here.
2. Always be truthful and kind; hold these virtues close to your heart.
3. Trust the Lord if you want a good reputation with God and humanity.
4. Trusting God will give you a reputation for good judgment and common sense.
5. Put God first, and he will crown your efforts with success.
6. Turn your back on evil, and you'll be given new health and vitality.
7. Honor the Lord by giving him the first part of your income; your barns will overflow with wheat and barley, and wine vats will overflow with the finest wines.
8. Welcome God's punishment; it is proof of his love.
9. Welcome God's punishment; the father punishes the son he delights in.
10. If you know right from wrong and have common sense and sound judgment, you will be happier than someone who is rich. Nothing compares to it.
11. Wisdom is more valuable than precious jewels; it leads you to a long, good life, riches, pleasure, honor, and peace.
12. Wisdom is the tree of life; if you eat from it, you will be happy.
13. Recognize that the Lord's wisdom and understanding founded the Earth, space, and universe.
14. Know that the Lord's knowledge broke out the fountain of the Earth and brought down the rain.
15. Have two goals—wisdom (knowing what's right) and common sense:
    A. Wisdom and common sense is a feather in the cap and helps you live with energy.
    B. Wisdom and common sense keep you safe and on the right trail.

    C. Wisdom and common sense keeps you from wicked plots and helps you sleep with no fear.

    D. Wisdom and common sense protect you from disasters.

16. Be godly; God gives his friendship to the godly.

17. There is a blessing for you if you are upright.

18. If you remain humble, you will be helped, and if you are wise, promoted to honor.

CHAPTER 3

What God Wants Us to Avoid

Chapter 3 reveals that people should not trust themselves over God and avoid copying others' negative behavior. Specifically, a wise person is not arrogant; he does not take his own counsel over God's instruction. He does not reject God over the correction he receives, for it was the human desire for knowledge that broke the foundation of Earth and brought the rain. He knows the very rich are less happy than those with basic common sense and good judgment, and the wealthy are less satisfied than those who know right from wrong. God warns his people not to copy the world's ways and not to envy or copy violent men, an absolute abomination to God. To avoid needless fights and any attempt to plot against one's neighbors, people should repay their debts as soon as possible. Finally, God reminds individuals that the wicked have a curse, mockers will be mocked, and the fools are promoted to shame.

Chapter 3
Key Points: Things to Avoid

1. Don't trust yourself.
2. Don't be conceited.
3. Avoid your own wisdom.
4. Do not shun or resent God's correction.
5. If you are rich, you will be less happy than those with common sense, good judgment, and knowing right from wrong.
6. Avoid the failure of not repaying debts.
7. Don't plot against your neighbor.
8. Don't get into needless fights.
9. Don't envy violent men.
10. Don't copy violent men, which is an abomination.
11. Don't be like the wicked who are cursed.
12. Avoid needless fights and violence.
13. Don't mock the godly or you will be mocked.
14. Don't be a fool or you will be promoted to shame.

CHAPTER 4

Things to Seek, Be, or Do

Chapter 4 emphasizes listening to mother, father, and God and energizing lives with wisdom. Specifically, individuals should seek the companionship of their earthly fathers and listen to their wisdom and embrace their mother's tender love. By listening to parents, they grow wise and speak the truth. To live a long and happy life, they must be careful and use the good judgment and common sense they acquire. Clinging to wisdom guards and protects them. Ultimately, as God reveals, if his followers exalt wisdom, they will be elevated, resulting in high honors and becoming a beautiful crown for those who obey this truth. How do people achieve the wisest life? Not by limping or stumbling along but by doing right, which is a sign of authentic living. For when a good man walks in God's favor, he walks in the ever-brightening light of God's blessings like the morning splendor of dawn. God reminds individuals to stick to the path and guard their affections because it influences everything in their lives. He implores people to keep all these thoughts in their hearts, and they will be rewarded with real and radiant life.

Chapter 4
Key Points: Things to Seek, Be, or Do

1. Listen to this word like you would your father and grow wise and have a long and happy life.
2. Speak the truth and never turn from it.
3. Learn to be wise and develop good judgment and common sense.
4. Cling to wisdom; it will protect you.
5. Exalt wisdom, and wisdom exalts you and brings you a crown and great honors.
6. Your wisest life is one of doing right, which leads to real living.
7. If you are a good person, you will walk in the bright light of God's favor.
8. Let these thoughts penetrate your heart, leading to radiant health and real life.
9. Guard your affections, for they influence everything in your life.
10. Stick to the path to be safe.

CHAPTER 4

What God Wants Us to Avoid

Chapter 4 warns people to avoid turning away from God and following the ways of the wicked. They are advised to stay away from these people's places and avoid eating and drinking with them. Why? Evil men don't sleep until they've done their evil deed for the day. They grope and stumble in the dark and won't rest until someone slips and falls with them, so avoid the side tracks of their path, for even the mere kiss of a prostitute brings danger.

Chapter 4
Key Points: Things to Avoid

1. Don't turn away from the truth.
2. Doing wrong leads to limping and stumbling.
3. Avoid what the wicked do; avoid where they hang out.
4. Avoid evil men who don't sleep until they have done evil.
5. Avoid evil men who won't rest until someone stumbles and falls.
6. Avoid evil men who eat and drink violence.
7. Don't be the evil man who gropes and stumbles in the dark.
8. Avoid the kiss of the prostitute.
9. Don't even look at the prostitute; look straight ahead.
10. Avoid sidetracks and keep your feet from danger.

CHAPTER 5

Things to Seek, Be, or Do

In Chapter 5, God talks about the joys of having a wife and, in direct contrast, to run from prostitutes. Specifically, a man should make his manhood a blessing by being faithful and true to his wife—to rejoice in the wife of his youth, to embrace her and delight in her charms and love. Finally, God states that he is watching people closely and weighs everything they do.

Chapter 5
Key Points: Things to Seek, Be, or Do

1. Run from prostitutes.
2. Be faithful and be true to your wife.
3. Rejoice in the wife of your youth and make your manhood a blessing.
4. Let your wife's charms, embrace, and love fill you with delight.
5. God is watching everything you do and weighs this carefully.

CHAPTER 5

What God Wants Us to Avoid

Chapter 5 explains the hefty penalty of being involved with prostitutes. Specifically, the flattery and honey lips of a prostitute cause one to be indiscreet and give away vital information. The temptation and crooked trail of the prostitute lead to death and hell. When a person engages with a prostitute, they lose honor and live a cruel, ruthless life. They lose wealth, become a slave to foreigners, groan in anguish and shame, and suffer from syphilis. They suffer even more if they get a prostitute pregnant and become a public disgrace. They wish they would have listened, but it is too late; they demanded their way and now must pay the price. Sin catches and holds them. So don't be the wicked man, doomed by sin, who refuses the truth, heads into folly, and eventually dies.

Chapter 5
Key Points: Things to Avoid

1. Don't be indiscreet; keep vital information to yourself.
2. Avoid the flattery and honey lips of a prostitute.
3. Avoid the prostitute, which equals death and hell.
4. Avoid the temptation of the prostitute who is on the crooked trail.
5. Run from the prostitute and stay away from her house.
6. If you fall into the temptation of the prostitute, you will lose honor and live a cruel and merciless life.
7. Being with a prostitute means you'll lose wealth and become a slave to foreigners.
8. Being with a prostitute will end in anguish and shame, suffering with syphilis.
9. Being with a prostitute leads to regret for refusing advice, demanding your way, and becoming a public disgrace.
10. Don't get the prostitute pregnant.
11. Don't be the wicked man doomed by sin who heads into folly and dies by refusing the truth.
12. Don't be the wicked man caught and held by sin.

CHAPTER 6

Things to Seek, Be, or Do

Chapter 6 emphasizes hard work and following the excellent advice of parents, specifically, to work hard like the ant who uses summer work to prepare for the winter. People are advised to obey their mothers and fathers, to follow their wise instructions, and take their advice to heart, for the counsel they share will keep their children safe. Every morning to evening, embracing parents' guidance will keep them from harm. A parent's advice is like a beam of light, shining into the dark corners of the mind, reminding their children to keep away from the flattery of the prostitute.

Chapter 6
Key Points: Things to Seek, Be, or Do

1. Work hard like the ant who has no king but works hard in the summer to gather food for the winter.
2. Obey your mother and father; take all their advice to heart.
3. The counsel of your mother and father day and night leads you and keeps you safe.
4. Embrace the instructions of your parents in the morning and guide your day like a beam of light.
5. Let the counsel of your parents keep you from the flattery of the prostitute.

CHAPTER 6

What God Wants Us to Avoid

Chapter 6 focuses on not being evil or lazy, engaging in adultery or seeking the comfort of a prostitute. It advises not to guarantee other people's debts and to get out of that arrangement as soon as possible. Individuals are to avoid excessive sleep, which causes poverty and destruction. They are not to be wicked, filled with a heart of rebellion who always think of evil and stir up discontentment. He is a liar who signals his true intentions with his eyes, feet, and fingers and will suddenly be destroyed beyond hope. God makes what he hates clear: being haughty (arrogant), lying, plotting evil, eager to do wrong, being a false witness, sowing discord, and committing murder. He reminds all that the beauty, flattery, and coyness of the prostitute will cost victims their lives. God gives a harsh warning for those who take another man's wife. He compares this to trying to hold fire against one's chest, walking on hot coals, and getting blisters, and that it won't go unpunished. This type of thievery will be fined seven times for what is stolen. The adulterer is called the utter fool, plagued with constant wounds and disgrace until he destroys his soul. God warns that there will be no mercy from the woman's furious husband because he cannot be bought off, and the adulterer will find no mercy in the vengeance from the husband.

Chapter 6
Key Points: Things to Avoid

1. Don't guarantee the debts of others; if you have done so, try to get out of it now.
2. Avoid excessive sleep that brings poverty and destroys you.
3. Don't be the wicked man with a heart full of rebellion, thinking of evil, who stirs up discontent and will be destroyed suddenly with no hope.
4. Avoid what God hates: those who lie, the haughty murderers, those who plot evil, those who are eager to do wrong, the false witness, and those who sow discord.
5. Don't lust for the beauty of a prostitute or be seduced by her flattery, which leads to poverty and will cost you your life.
6. Avoid being with someone else's wife, which will punish and is like blisters from walking on coals or holding fire to your chest.
7. Compared to the adulterer, if you are a thief, you may be fined seven times what you stole, even if you have to sell your house.
8. If you commit adultery, you are like the utter fools who destroy their souls.
9. If you sleep with someone's wife, her husband will be angry with jealousy, and he will have no mercy, and you won't be able to buy him off.

CHAPTER 7

Things to Seek, Be, or Do

Chapter 7 advises readers to listen to inspired guidance, obey the heavenly father, write down and guard his words like a precious possession, and keep them in their hearts. They are told to embrace wisdom like a sweetheart or beloved family member and to reject the flattery of the prostitute. When people listen to and obey the wisdom that God gives, they don't even think about the prostitute and can keep their desires in check. They win this battle when they stay away from the temptation and seduction of the prostitute. They must not go near her and stay far away from where she walks.

Chapter 7
Key Points: Things to Seek, Be, or Do

1. Guard the advice from your father like a prized possession.
2. Obey your father, write down his words, take them to heart, and live.
3. Love wisdom like a sweetheart and a beloved family member.
4. Let wisdom keep you from prostitutes.
5. Obey my instructions and keep your desires in check.

CHAPTER 7

What God Wants Us to Avoid

Chapter 7 maintains a heavy emphasis on avoiding prostitutes. The temptation is strong, as women seduce with pretty speech and coaxing, destroying men like an ox going to a butcher, a deer trapped waiting for an arrow, or a bird flying into a snare. These women stand on street corners, dressed seductively, using flattery, and promising the most beautiful colored sheets from Egypt, each layer perfumed with myrrh, aloe, and cinnamon. Some of these women are married, promising a night of pleasure while their husbands are away. However, God gives anyone who succumbs to their charms a stark warning. Multitudes of men have become victims, and if they want to find the road to hell, they should look for the prostitute's house.

Chapter 7
Key Points: Things to Avoid

1. Avoid the seductions of the prostitute,

    A. The street corners where she solicits,
    B. Her seductive dressing,
    C. The promise of the finest colored sheets perfumed with myrrh, aloe, and cinnamon,
    D. Her flattery, seductive speech, and promise of a nighttime of pleasure, and
    E. Sending her husband away for several days to be alone.

2. Falling for a prostitute is like an ox going to the butcher, the deer trapped waiting for an arrow, or a bird trapped in the snare.
3. Avoid where the prostitute walks, where a host of men have been her victims.
4. Don't think about the prostitute; stay from the temptation and seduction.
5. If you want to find the road to hell, find the house of the prostitute.

CHAPTER 8

Things to Seek, Be, or Do

Chapter 8 relies heavily on the importance and definition of wisdom, which is essential and gives understanding and common sense. It hates lies and deception and loves what is right and true. Wisdom is described as wholesome and good with no evil, more valuable than gold or silver, and even more magnificent than rubies. Wisdom and judgment live together and rely on each other. Wisdom finds knowledge and understanding. It teaches one to fear God and to hate evil, pride, arrogance, deceit, and corruption of every kind. Wisdom is a giver and helper; famous for sound advice and common sense. It helps rulers lead well and gives king's power. It loves all who love it and is found by those seeking it. Unending riches and honor, justice, and righteousness are all distributed by wisdom. Those who follow wisdom will be wealthy; their treasuries will fill and overflow. A romantic picture of wisdom springs forth. Specifically, wisdom existed before creation, before the Earth and the oceans were formed, before springs bubbled up, before hills and mountains were created, and before God created fields and high plateaus. Wisdom was here when the heavens were formed, and great springs came up from the oceans. Wisdom told the seas not to go beyond its boundaries and was the blueprint for the Earth and the sea. Wisdom was at God's side like a child laughing, playing, and delighting in his presence. Wisdom was happy with the world God created and his family of mankind. Delighted is a man who seeks wisdom and watches at his gate or home for it. Therefore, whoever finds wisdom finds life and wins approval from the Lord.

Chapter 8
Key Points: Things to Seek, Be, or Do

1. Listen to the voice of wisdom, which

    A. Is always right and true and gives good advice;
    B. Gives understanding and common sense;
    C. Hates lies, deception, pride, arrogance, corruption, and deceit of every kind;
    D. Is wholesome and good;
    E. Has no evil in it;
    F. Is clear to everyone with even half a mind;
    G. Is more valuable than gold, silver, and rubies;
    H. Has nothing to which it can be compared
    I. Loves all who love it; and
    J. Is found by those seeking it.

2. Wisdom and good judgment live together.
3. Wisdom finds knowledge and understanding.
4. Wisdom hates pride, arrogance, corruption, and deceit of every kind.
5. Wisdom helps you respect and fear God and hate evil.
6. Wisdom gives kings power and the ability to rule well.
7. Wisdom gives unending riches, honor, justice, and righteousness.
8. Those who follow wisdom are wealthy, and their treasuries are filled.
9. Wisdom has been here forever

    A. Before anything was created,
    B. Before Earth began,
    C. Before oceans were created and springs bubbled up,
    D. Before mountains and hills were created,
    E. Before fields and high plateaus were created,
    F. Before heaven was formed,

G. Before great springs in the depth of oceans were created,

H. Before the seas were instructed not to go beyond their boundaries, and

I. Before the blueprint of Earth and oceans was created.

10. Wisdom is like the child at your side, laughing, playing, and delighting in your presence.

11. How happy God is with the world he created and the family of mankind.

12. How happy are the young men who listen to the instructions of wisdom.

13. If you seek wisdom, you will be happy.

14. You will be happy if you watch for wisdom daily at the gates of your home.

15. If you find wisdom, you will find life and win approval from the Lord.

CHAPTER 8

What God Wants Us to Avoid

Chapter 8 provides some specific points on what not to do. First, people are to avoid lies, deception, and evil. They should come to hate evil, knowing the damage it can do. They are encouraged to prevent pride, arrogance, corruption, and deceit of every kind. Next, wisdom is again mentioned prominently, and those who miss wisdom are injured irreparably, for the refusal of wisdom means to love death. Finally, they are to embrace wisdom and avoid the opposite of it.

Chapter 8
Key: Things to Avoid

1. Avoid lies and deception.
2. Avoid and hate evil.
3. Avoid pride, arrogance, corruption, and deceit of every kind.
4. Avoid missing wisdom, or you will be injured irreparably.
5. If you refuse wisdom, you love death.

CHAPTER 9

Things to Seek, Be, or Do

Chapter 9's central theme once again is wisdom. Specifically, an invitation is given for it, and its benefits are emphasized. Wisdom is described as readily available to all, like a great banquet with the most excellent wines to be shared, with many maidens giving out invitations on the busiest of streets to those who don't have it. Those who are smart enough to replace foolishness with wisdom gain life. There are clues that a man has become wiser, for a wise man rebuked will love you more, and a wise man open to being taught becomes even more intelligent and will learn more. Reverence and the fear of God are the basis for all wisdom, and knowing God results in all understanding. Wisdom is its own reward; it makes the days more profitable and the years of life more fruitful.

Chapter 9
Key Points: Things to Seek, Be, or Do

1. Wisdom is like a palace built on seven pillars.
2. Wisdom is like a great banquet with the finest wines.
3. Wisdom is like the maidens at the city intersection inviting them in.
4. Wisdom says, "Come to the banquet, drink the wine, leave foolishness behind."
5. Wisdom says, "Learn how to live and be wise."
6. Wisdom is life.
7. The wise man rebuked will love more.
8. A wise man who welcomes teaching becomes wiser.
9. Teach a good man, and he will learn more.
10. Reverence and fear of God are the basis for all wisdom.
11. Knowing God results in all understanding.
12. Wisdom makes the hours of the day more profitable.
13. Wisdom makes years of life more fruitful.
14. Wisdom is its own reward.

CHAPTER 9

What God Wants Us to Avoid

Chapter 9 shows that scorning or ignoring wisdom can only hurt a person with foolishness and poor judgment as the end result. People are advised to avoid these mockers who snarl and respond with smart retorts and who only hate others for trying to help them. Another picture of a prostitute is described. She is on the street corner or near the door of her house, calling out to men. She is loud and brash and never has enough of lust and shame and whispers to men trying to mind their own business, "Come home with me; stolen melons are the sweetest, and stolen apples taste the best." However, all her former guests are now citizens of hell.

Chapter 10
Key Points: Things to Avoid

1. You will be sad if you are the mother of a rebel.
2. Don't be wicked or your riches won't continue.
3. If you have ill-gotten gain, your happiness will be short.
4. If you're lazy, you will be poor, and it is a shame to sleep away opportunity.
5. If you're evil, you will curse your own luck.
6. If you're wicked, your name will stink.
7. Don't be a self-sufficient fool or you'll fall flat on your face.
8. If you're a crook, you will slip and fall.
9. If you wink at sin, it will lead to sorrow.
10. Your mouth will be filled with curses if you're evil.
11. Your hatred will stir old quarrels.
12. You will be beaten as a servant if you have no common sense.
13. Don't be a fool who blurts out everything you know, leading to sorrow and trouble.
14. If you're rich, your wealth is your only strength.
15. Don't be evil and squander your money on sin.
16. If you're evil and refuse to be corrected, you will lose your chance.
17. Hating will make you a liar.
18. Slandering will make you a fool.
19. Over-talking is like putting your foot in your mouth.
20. The words of a fool are seen as plentiful but have no value.
21. A lack of common sense will destroy you if you're a rebel.
22. If you're a fool, your fun is being bad.
23. A wicked man's fears come true.
24. Disaster strikes like a cyclone, and if you are wicked, you'll be whirled away.
25. If you're lazy, you will be a pain to your employer—like smoke in the eyes or vinegar on the teeth.

26. If you are wicked, you don't revere God, which means you can't expect a good, long life.
27. Your hopes are all in vain if you are evil.
28. Be warned: God destroys the wicked, and you will lose everything.
29. If you are a liar, your counsel and advice are shunned.
30. If you are wicked, you will always speak rebellion.

CHAPTER 11

Things to Seek, Be, or Do

Chapter 11 brings a description of the godly man and good people. These are the human beings that the Lord delights in because they are guided by honesty. All upright people are directed by honesty. God rescues and delivers the good man from danger, and because the meek become wise, their righteousness counts on judgment day. The whole city celebrates a good man's godly skill and success, and these godly citizens rebuild it and cause it to prosper. A man with good sense holds his tongue, a trustworthy man quiets rumors, and good counselors provide safety. Honors go to kind and gracious women, as everyone's soul is nourished when they are kind. The good man finds life, he looks forward to happiness, and his rewards last forever. God rescues the godly children, and he delights in those who are good. The good people are also givers. The giver becomes rich, for when he waters others, he gives water to himself. People bless those who sell to them in time of need, and therefore, it is possible to give away and get richer. God is our guide. When you search for him, you find God's favor, and when you trust in God, you will flourish like a tree. Godly men bear life-giving fruit, for all who win souls are wise.

Chapter 11
Key Points: Things to Seek, Be, or Do

1. Honesty guides you if you're good and upright, and the Lord delights in this.
2. Be meek and become wise; righteousness counts on judgment day.
3. Goodness delivers you if you're a good man, and God rescues the good from danger.
4. If you're a good man, the whole city celebrates your success.
5. Your godly skill rebuilds, and godly citizens cause the city to prosper.
6. If you have good sense, you'll hold your tongue; the trustworthy person quiets rumors.
7. You will find safety in good counselors.
8. Be kind and gracious women, and you'll receive honors.
9. Your soul is nourished when you are kind.
10. Be good and your rewards will last forever, and you will find life.
11. God delights in you if you're good, and he rescues the godly children.
12. As a good person, you will look forward to happiness.
13. It's possible for you to give away and get richer.
14. As a giver you will become rich because when you water others, you water yourself.
15. People bless those who sell to others in a time of need.
16. When you search for God, you find God's favor.
17. Trust in God and flourish like a tree.
18. Be a godly man and bear life-giving fruit.
19. If you win souls, you are wise.

CHAPTER 11

What God Wants Us to Avoid

Chapter 11 is a mixed bag of things to avoid, specifically wicked things. The Lord hates cheating, and evil men are destroyed by dishonesty. These proud men end in shame because their riches won't matter on judgment day. These wicked men are undone by their treachery and fall below a load of sins. Their hopes perish when they die because they are based on earthly life. God lets the wicked man fall into danger; his evil words are used to destroy, and the moral decay that arises drives the city downhill, and, eventually, the city celebrates the godless man's death. Be wise, for a nation is in trouble without wise leadership as the gossipers speak rumors and have foolish quarrels with neighbors. Mere money is cruel men's only honor, and others struggle because they vouch for the credit of people they hardly know. These evil men only get rich for the moment. The Lord hates stubborn people, and the souls of the cruel are destroyed. The evil man is eventually punished and finds death. Even the beautiful woman who lacks discretion and modesty is like a gold ring attached to a pig's nose. The wicked can expect wrath, and it's possible to hold on tightly to what they have and still lose everything. People curse sellers who want a higher price for their grain and those who only trust in their money, and watch, down they go! Those who search for evil find God's curse, and the fool who provokes his family with anger and resentment will have nothing left and will be a servant to a wiser man. Even the godly are rewarded on earth, so how much more the wicked!

CHAPTER 12

Things to Seek, Be, or Do

The godly can benefit from various positive attributes described in Chapter 12. Specifically, to learn, they must want to be taught to realize that God blesses good men whose minds are filled with honest thoughts, and everyone admires the man who has good sense. Only the godly have real success because they defend in the face of accusation, and for this reason, they stand tall. Family is important, and God says that the husband who finds a worthy wife finds his joy and crown. Hard work returns many blessings; it is the sign of a leader and means prosperity. Good men long to help others, for getting their hands dirty means they get to eat! A good man is concerned about the welfare of animals. Honesty becomes its own defense, and the good man is known for his truthfulness. Truth brings excellent satisfaction because it stands the test of time. The wise man is careful with his words; he listens to others and stays calm when insulted. A wise man doesn't display his knowledge to impress but uses his words for encouragement. It works wonders to soothe, heal, and keep the peace. The diligent and good man uses everything he finds and asks for advice from his friends. Joy fills the hearts of those planning good, and no actual harm comes to them. God loves those who keep their promises, and the path of the godly leads to life.

Chapter 12
Key Points: Things to Seek, Be, or Do

1. To learn, you must want to be taught.
2. Be godly because the godly shall stand, the godly shall defend, and only the godly have real success.
3. Be good and the Lord will bless you.
4. Be a worthy wife, your husband's joy and crown.
5. If you're a good man, your mind is filled with honest thoughts, and everyone admires a man with good sense.
6. Work hard, get your hands dirty and eat; hard work means prosperity and many blessings.
7. Be a good man who is concerned for the welfare of animals.
8. Be the good man who longs to help one another.
9. Honesty is its own defense, so telling the truth is your great satisfaction.
10. Be wise and listen to others and stay calm when you're insulted.
11. As a good man, you'll be known for truthfulness and stand the test of time.
12. Be wise and your words will soothe and heal, and no harm befalls the good.
13. Joy fills your hearts when planning good, and God loves those who keep promises.
14. When you are wise, you don't display knowledge but know words of encouragement works wonders.
15. Work hard and become a leader.
16. Be good and ask for advice from friends; be diligent and use everything you find.
17. Be godly and your path will lead to life.

CHAPTER 12

What God Wants Us to Avoid

Chapter 12 has a heavy emphasis on the dangers of wickedness. Specifically, the wicked plunge ahead and fall and face constant trouble. The corrupt accuse others but never have any real success, and because the Lord condemns them, they shall perish. The evil man's mind is crammed full of lies, and because he refuses reproof, he is stupid. He is despised because he has a warped mind. These fools are quick-tempered and think they need no advice. These are lazy men who never succeed; fools that idle their time away and are too proud to work. Even if these "hunters" catch something, they are too lazy to prepare it, so they starve. These crooks are jealous of each other's loot, and deceit fills the hearts of those plotting evil. These false men make cutting remarks and are known for their fraud and lies, which are soon exposed. Even the "kindness" of godless men is cruel. The unworthy wife destroys her husband's strength and tears down everything he does. God hates those who lie and don't keep their promises. These fools display their foolishness, and their anxious hearts are heavy because these godless people fear their own deaths.

Chapter 12
Key Points: Things to Avoid

1. Don't refuse reproof, which is stupid.
2. If you are wicked, the Lord will condemn you, and you will never have real success.
3. Don't be an unworthy wife who corrodes her husband's strength and tears down everything he does.
4. Don't be an evil person whose mind is full of lies.
5. Don't be wicked or accuse others and perish.
6. If you have a warped mind, you will be despised.
7. Don't be foolish and idle your time away, and if you're too proud to work, you'll starve.
8. Even your kindness is cruel if you are godless.
9. Don't be a crook, being rebellious and jealous of other crooks' loot.
10. If you lie, you'll get into trouble.
11. Don't be a fool who is quick-tempered and thinks he needs no advice.
12. If you are false, you'll be known for deceit, lies, and cutting remarks.
13. If you plot evil, deceit fills your heart, and lies are soon exposed.
14. If you're wicked, you will have constant trouble, as the fool displays his foolishness.
15. Keep your promises because God hates those who don't keep them.
16. Be lazy and you'll never succeed.
17. Your anxious heart will be heavy.
18. Don't be wicked or you'll plunge ahead and fall.
19. Don't be a lazy hunter who won't prepare what you catch.
20. If you're godless, you'll fear death.

CHAPTER 13

Things to Seek, Be, or Do

Chapter 13 touches on positive attributes and clever tips. Excellent communication, helping the poor, success, parenting, and becoming wise are among those things included. Specifically, we learn that a good man wins a debate by careful argument, hating all lies, and understanding that self-control includes the tongue. He knows that reliable communication is key to all progress, and since he accepts criticism, he is on the road to fame. Money does not equate to success, for being kidnapped and held for ransom never worries the poor, and because of this, some poor people have great wealth. Wisdom starts early. If a man loves his son, he will promptly punish him, and the son, wanting to be wise, readily accepts his father's punishment. When he dies, the man leaves an inheritance for his children. The wise man thinks ahead and is appreciated, and his wisdom refreshes like a mountain spring; he spends his time with wise men to gather more wisdom to share. The humble take advice and become wiser! They are enlightened and wary of future pitfalls. We learn we must be diligent in becoming prosperous, and if we obey God's word, we shall succeed. The man who eats to live watches the wealth from his hard work grow. Seeing his plans develop and his existence is full of life is pleasant. Because blessings chase the righteous, his dreams come true, and he can find a meaningful and joyful life.

Chapter 13
Key Points: Things to Seek, Be, or Do"

1. Be wise in your youth and accept your father's rebuke.
2. The good man wins his case by careful argument.
3. Your self-control means the tongue.
4. Be diligent and you will prosper.
5. If you are good, you will hate lies.
6. You may be poor but have great wealth.
7. Being kidnapped and held for ransom never worries you if you are poor.
8. Your life will be full of light if you're a good person.
9. Be humble so that you may take advice and become wise.
10. Your hard work grows wealth.
11. When your dreams come true, you'll have life and joy. Obey God's word and succeed.
12. Be wise and think ahead; your advice refreshes like a mountain spring.
13. If you have good sense, you will be appreciated.
14. Your reliable communication permits progress.
15. Accept criticism and be on the road to fame.
16. It's pleasant to see your plans develop.
17. Be with wise men and become wise.
18. Blessings chase you if you're righteous.
19. If you're a good man, when you die, you'll leave an inheritance for your children.
20. If you love your son, be prompt to punish him.
21. Being good means eating to live.

CHAPTER 13

What God Wants Us to Avoid

In Chapter 13, we see little hope for those who mock God. Who are they? These people struggle with communication and shame themselves with constant lying. They are evil-minded and often ruin everything with a quick retort. Their pride leads to needless arguments and fights. These unreliable messengers halt progress; they refuse to take criticism and end up in poverty and disgrace. The mocker finds no success; they are lazy people who achieve little but still live to eat. Their wealth from gambling soon disappears, and those rich with money are poor in spirit. Even the poor, who have good soil, are robbed of their riches because of their injustice. All seems hopeless for this sinner, and his wealth is stored up for the godly when he dies. His own young son refuses his father's punishment, and because his father doesn't discipline him, he shows he does not love him. The sinner's road is dark and gloomy; they walk a treacherous and rocky road. He is the fool who refuses to give up on his evil plans. He doesn't think ahead and even brags about it. These men spend time with evil men and become eviler. Their curses attract other sinners, and their hope deferred makes the heart sick. They despise God's word and find themselves in serious trouble.

Chapter 13
Key Points: Things to Avoid

1. Don't be a young mocker who refuses his father's rebuke.
2. Don't be an evil-minded person who only wants to fight.
3. Your your quick retort ruins everything.
4. Don't be lazy and want things but get little.
5. If you are wicked, you will shame yourself by lying constantly.
6. You can be rich yet poor.
7. The sinner's road is dark and gloomy.
8. Your pride leads to arguments.
9. If you gain wealth from gambling, it will disappear.
10. Hope deferred makes your heart sick.
11. Despise God's word and find yourself in trouble.
12. Don't be treacherous or you'll walk a rocky road.
13. Don't be a fool who doesn't think ahead and even brags about it.
14. Don't be an unreliable messenger who halts progress.
15. Refuse criticism, and it ends in poverty and disgrace.
16. Don't be a fool who refuses to give up on wrong plans.
17. Be with evil men and become evil.
18. Don't be a sinner because curses will chase after you.
19. If you are a sinner, when you die, your wealth will be stored up for the godly.
20. Refusing to discipline your son means you don't love him.
21. If you are poor, your farm has good soil, but injustice robs you of riches.
22. Being evil means living to eat.

CHAPTER 14

Things to Seek, Be, or Do

In Chapter 14, we see that a wise woman builds up her house and that a wise man's speech is respected because he never lies. The truth-telling witness saves good men from death. The wise man uses common sense, looks ahead, and stays away from fools. The wise man is a patient and prudent man who checks to see where he is going. He is crowned with knowledge and controls his temper as he knows anger causes mistakes. He is cautious and avoids danger. Wisdom sits in the hearts of men with common sense, so they are praised for their understanding. Godly people bond over the goodwill they do, and they do right to honor God. The divine will flourish, and the godly man's life is exciting. They are kind, knowing only the person involved knows the joy or bitterness. The godly are blessed, for they show pity and help the poor, which honors God. The godly plan well; they receive quietness and mercy. Their hard work brings profit, and if their attitude is relaxed, it will lengthen their life. Reverence for God gives a man remarkable strength; it is like a fountain of life to keep him from death and is a place of refuge and security for his children. A king's greatest glories are servants who know what to do and a growing population. Because the godly help exalt the nation, they have a refuge when they die.

CHAPTER 15

Things to Seek, Be, or Do

Chapter 15 reveals that God saw in his wisdom the importance of communication to our existence, health, and ability to prosper or perish. A soft answer turns away wrath, and gentle words enhance life and health. We further see that only the good can give good advice. This is why the wise son considers each suggestion from his father, and the sensible son gladdens his father. Communication is an art, and the Lord delights in kind words. If we intelligently use constructive criticism, we should be elected to the wise man's hall of fame! It is a wonderful feeling to say the right thing at the right time, and we help others and help ourselves when we do this! Therefore, the good man thinks before he speaks. We learn the Lord is watching the good; he delights in the people's prayers and hears the righteous prayers. The Lord loves those who try to be good. The wise teacher makes learning a joy and opens the hearts of mankind to God's knowledge. A wise man is simply hungry for the truth and enjoys good advice. Following wise advice, the good man's path becomes easy. His happy face means a glad heart. For when a man is cheerful, everything seems right! The wise man knows it is better to be poor and own little as long as he has a reverence for God. His calm temper stops fights, and he has the wisdom to know that soup with a friend is better than steak with an enemy. He knows many counselors bring success, and he stays on the pathway of the right. He understands that hating bribes brings happiness. He watches as the Lord cares for widows, and he knows the road of the godly leads upward, leaving hell behind. He embraces the pleasant sights and good reports, knowing that an excellent account gives happiness and health. Lastly, he understands humility and reference for the Lord will make him both wise and honored.

Chapter 15
Key Points: Things to Seek, Be, or Do

1. Your soft answer turns away wrath.
2. Be a wise teacher who makes learning a joy.
3. Be good, for the Lord is watching.
4. Your gentle words cause life and health.
5. Be a wise son who considers each suggestion from your father.
6. You can only give good advice if you are good.
7. The Lord delights in your prayers.
8. The Lord loves you if you try to be good.
9. His word opens your heart to God's knowledge.
10. Your happy face indicates a glad heart.
11. Be wise and hungry for the truth.
12. When you are cheerful, everything seems right!
13. It is better for you to have little but have reverence for God.
14. It is better to have soup with someone else than steak with someone you hate.
15. Be cool-tempered and stop fights.
16. If you're a good person, your path will be easy.
17. If you're a sensible son, you will gladden your father.
18. Be sensible and stay on the right path; many counselors bring success.
19. Everyone enjoys good advice, and it is wonderful if you say the right thing at the right time.
20. The road of the godly leads upward, leaving hell behind.
21. The Lord delights in kind words, and if you're good, you'll think before you speak.
22. Your hate for bribes brings happiness.
23. Be righteous and the Lord will hear your prayers.
24. Pleasant sights and good reports bring you happiness and health.
25. Use constructive criticism and be elected to the wise man's hall of fame.
26. Humility and reverence for the Lord will make you both wise and honored.

CHAPTER 15

What God Wants Us to Avoid

Chapter 15 also shows communication can destroy. Hard words cause quarrels. Griping causes discouragement. A rebel can't give good advice, and a rebellious teacher spouts foolishness. A fool even despises his father's advice. These wicked people reject constructive criticism and harm themselves and their own interests. The Lord is watching this evil; he despises the gifts and deeds of the wicked. These mockers stay away from wise men because they hate to be scolded. They reject God's knowledge, so the depths of hell are open to them. This rebel stops trying to be good, so the Lord punishes him, and he dies. He has a sad face from his breaking heart and feeds on lies; when a man becomes gloomy, everything seems to go wrong. His dishonest money brings grief to the family. His great treasure only brings trouble because he has no reverence for God, so the Lord destroys the possessions of those who are proud. These rebels sadden their mother. They are quick-tempered and start fights. He eats steak with his enemies and enjoys the folly, which shows something is wrong. He is a lazy fellow who has trouble all through his life. This evil man pours out the evil before thinking, but the Lord hates these thoughts because God is far from the wicked.

Chapter 15
Key Points: Things to Avoid

1. Your hard words cause quarrels.
2. Don't be a rebellious teacher who spouts foolishness.
3. Don't be evil, for the Lord is watching you.
4. If you complain about things, you cause discouragement.
5. Don't be a fool and despise your father's advice.
6. If you're a rebel, you can't give good advice.
7. Don't be wicked or the Lord will hate your gifts.
8. Don't be wicked or the Lord will despise your deeds.
9. Don't stop being good, for the Lord will punish you.
10. If you rebel against God, you will die.
11. Even the depths of hell are open to knowledge, even more to your heart, but will you take it?
12. The mocker stays away from wise men because they hate to be scolded.
13. Your sad face means a breaking heart.
14. Don't be a mocker who feeds on the trash of lies.
15. Don't be gloomy, for everything seems to go wrong.
16. You will have trouble with great treasure if you have no reverence for God.
17. Having steak with someone you hate is worse than having soup with someone you like.
18. If you are quick-tempered, you will start fights.
19. If you're lazy, you'll have trouble all through your life.
20. If you are rebellious, you will sadden your mother.
21. If you enjoy folly, something is wrong.
22. If you have too few counselors, your plans will go wrong.
23. Don't be proud or the Lord will destroy your possessions.
24. Don't be wicked, for the Lord will hate your thoughts.
25. If you have dishonest money, it will bring grief to your family.
26. Don't be evil and pour out evil words before thinking.
27. If you are wicked, the Lord is far from you.
28. Reject criticism and you will harm yourself and your own interests.

CHAPTER 16

Things to Seek, Be, or Do

Chapter 16 reminds them that God is in control, and though they make plans, the final outcome is in God's hands. No matter one's desires, the Lord has made everything for his purpose, and when people commit their work to God, it will succeed, so they should make their plans counting on God to help them. They may toss the coin, but God controls the decision. Following the Lord is the wise path, for when a man is trying to please God, his worst enemies are at peace with him; the Lord keeps him safe and leads him away from evil. God will help the king judge the people fairly and make no mistakes. The king's right to rule will depend on his fairness, and the king himself rejoices when people are truthful and fair. The wise man appeases the king when he is angry, for many favors are showered upon those who please the king. Truly being good comes from reverence for God, as he blesses those who obey him. His mercy and truth atone for their iniquity. God wants them to master the basics; he demands fairness in every business deal. He teaches them that little gained with honesty is better than wealth attained with dishonesty. God shows us it is better to be poor and humble than rich and proud. Happy is the man who trusts in the Lord. His wisdom is better than gold, and understanding is better than silver. Wisdom shows them it's better to be slow-tempered than famous; it's better to have self-control than control an army. Hunger is good if it makes them work. The wise man produces careful and persuasive speech; kind words are like honey—enjoyable and healthful. A pleasant teacher is the best, and the wise man is known for his common sense. White hair is the crown of glory seen on the godly. Wisdom is the fountain of life.

Chapter 16
Key Points: Things to Seek, Be, or Do

1. You make plans, but the final outcome is in God's hands.
2. Commit your work to God, and then it will succeed.
3. Follow the Lord, he has made everything for his purposes.
4. If you are truly good, it comes from reverence for God.
5. Gross injustice done to you is atoned for by mercy and truth.
6. When you are trying to please God, your worse enemies are at peace with you.
7. Your small honest gain is better than dishonest wealth.
8. You should make plans, counting on God to help you.
9. You will be judged by the king, watch your step, there will be no mistakes.
10. The Lord demands fairness in all your business deals.
11. Appease the king, for his right to rule, depends on his fairness.
12. When you are truthful and fair, the king rejoices.
13. Be the wise man who appeases the anger of the king.
14. Please the king and he will shower you with favors.
15. If you have wisdom, it is better than gold; understanding better than silver.
16. If you're godly, your path is safe because it leads away from evil.
17. It is better for you to be poor and humble than the opposite.
18. God blesses you if you obey him.
19. You will be happy if you trust in the Lord.
20. Be wise and you will be known for your common sense.
21. Be a pleasant teacher and you will be the best teacher.
22. Be wise, for wisdom is the fountain of life.
23. If you have a wise mind, it will produce careful and persuasive speech.
24. Your kind words are honey and enjoyable and healthful.
25. Hunger is good if it makes you work.

26. Your white hair is a crown of glory seen on the godly.
27. It is better for you to be slow-tempered than famous.
28. It is better for you to have self-control than to control an army.
29. We toss the coin, but God controls the decision.

CHAPTER 16

What God Wants Us to Avoid

Chapter 16 shows them they can make their own plans and try to prove they are right, but is God convinced? The Lord has made rebels and the wicked for punishment. Stirring the anger of the king is like the messenger of death, and it is a horrible thing for a king to do evil. Pride disgusts the Lord, and he shall punish proud men. Pride goes before destruction and haughtiness before a fall. They are proud of their wealth acquired through dishonesty. They would rather be proud and rich than poor and humble. Before every lost man lies a wide and pleasant road that ends in death. His idle hands are the devil's workshop, his idle lips are the devil's mouthpiece, and a gossip separates the best of friends. The evil man sows strife, and a fool's burden is his folly. These wicked men stare into space with pursed lips, deep in thought planning evil deeds. Their wickedness loves company, and he leads others into sin.

Chapter 16
Key Points: Things to Avoid

1. We can prove we are right, but is God convinced?
2. Don't be wicked, for the Lord has made the wicked for punishment.
3. Don't be proud, for pride disgusts the Lord.
4. It's worse for you to attain wealth through dishonesty than the opposite.
5. Beware the horrible king who does evil things.
6. Don't stir the king to anger; he is the messenger of death.
7. Your pride goes before destruction; haughtiness before the fall.
8. It is better for you to be poor and humble than proud and rich.
9. Don't be a fool whose burden is folly.
10. Before every person lies a wide and pleasant road, but it ends in death.
11. Your idle hands are the devil's workshop.
12. Your idle lips are the devil's mouthpiece.
13. The evil man sows strife.
14. Your gossip will separate you from the best of friends.
15. Wickedness loves company; don't let it lead you into sin.
16. Don't be a wicked person who stares into space, deep in thought, planning evil deeds.

CHAPTER 17

Things to Seek, Be, or Do

Chapter 17 explains that keeping the peace is imperative, as they are reminded once again that a dry crust eaten in peace is better than eating a steak every day where there is argument and strife. A child's glory is his father, and an older man's grandchildren are his crowning glory. But they should take heed, for even a wise slave will ruin his wicked sons and share his master's estate. Life is about the heart, for while silver and gold are purified by fire, God purifies hearts. Love forgets mistakes, a true friend is always loyal, and a brother is born to help in time of need. A cheerful heart does good like medicine, and a bribe works like magic; whoever uses it for good will prosper. Wisdom is the primary pursuit of sensible men. The settled man of few words is wise. Even a fool is thought to be wise when silent; it pays to keep the mouth shut.

Chapter 17
Key Points: Things to Seek, Be, or Do

1. Eating a dry crust of bread is better for you than a steak eaten in strife.
2. If you are a wise slave, you will rule your master's wicked sons and share their estate.
3. Don't worry about silver and gold; let God purify your heart.
4. Your grandchildren are the crowning glory of their grandfather.
5. As a child, your glory is your father.
6. A bribe works like magic; if you use it for good, you will prosper.
7. If you love, you will forget mistakes.
8. Your rebuke to someone with common sense is effective.
9. Your true friend will always be loyal.
10. Your brother is born to help you in time of need.
11. Your cheerful heart is like good medicine.
12. If you are sensible, wisdom is your primary pursuit.
13. If you use few words and have a settled mind, you are wise; even a fool is thought to be wise when silent.
14. It pays to keep your mouth shut.

CHAPTER 17

What God Wants Us to Avoid

Chapter 17 explains that the wicked would rather eat steak amid strife and argument than a crust of bread in peace. They enjoy fellowship with others who are evil; these lazy liars enjoy other liars. They mock God because they mock the poor, but God punishes those who rejoice at others' misfortunes. While lies from the king are unexpected, the truth from the rebel is also shocking. They lose their best friends because they nag them about their mistakes, and once the quarrel starts, it is hard to stop. They should know not to let the argument even begin. They boast, look for trouble, use poor judgment in signing notes, and are responsible for others' debts. It's no fun being a rebel's father. His son brings him grief and is a bitter blow to his mother. These sinners love to fight and giving them a wise rebuke is as effective as providing 100 lashes to their backs. They only see the pain, live for rebellion, and will be severely punished. It's senseless to pay tuition to educate a rebel with no heart for the truth; it's safer to meet a bear robbed of her cubs than a rebellious fool caught in his folly. The evil man is suspicious of everyone and tumbles into constant trouble. Their broken spirit makes them sick. These fools' goals are at the end of the earth. People should be wise; if they repay evil for good, a curse is upon their head. It is wrong to accept bribes to twist justice, and it is short-sighted to fine the godly for being good or to punish the noble for being honest. The Lord despises those who say that bad is good and good is bad.

Chapter 17
Key Points: Things to Avoid

1. Eating steak in strife is worse than your eating bread in peace.
2. Don't be wicked and enjoy fellowship with others who are wicked.
3. Don't be a liar who enjoys other liars.
4. If you mock the poor, you are mocking God.
5. Don't rejoice at others' misfortunes, for God will punish you.
6. Don't be the rebel where the truth is unexpected. Instead, be more like the truthful king, where lies are unexpected.
7. Don't nag about mistakes because it parts the best of friends.
8. Don't be the rebel who needs 100 lashes to the back before he hears a rebuke.
9. Don't be like the wicked who live for rebellion and shall be severely punished.
10. It's safer for you to meet a bear robbed of her cubs than a fool caught in his folly.
11. If you repay evil for good, a curse is upon your head.
12. It's hard to stop a quarrel once it starts, so don't let it begin.
13. The Lord despises you if you say that bad is good and good is bad.
14. It's senseless for you to pay tuition to educate the rebel with no heart for the truth.
15. Don't sign a note and be responsible for others' debts; it shows poor judgment.
16. Don't be a sinner who loves to fight.
17. If you boast, you're looking for trouble.
18. If you are evil, you are suspicious of everyone and tumble into constant trouble.
19. It's no fun for you to be a rebel's father.
20. A broken spirit will make you sick.

21. It's wrong for you to accept a bribe to twist justice.
22. If you are a fool, your goals are at the end of the earth.
23. Don't be a rebellious son who is a grief to his father and a bitter blow to his mother.
24. It is short-sighted for you to fine the godly for being good or punish the nobles for being honest.

CHAPTER 18

Things to Seek, Be, or Do

Chapter 18 shows that deep streams of good thoughts come from a wise man's words. His advice satisfies like a good meal. The poor man pleads, and a coin toss against powerful opponents ends arguments. A bribe does wonders before important men. The godly run to the Lord, for he is a strong fortress and keeps them safe. Humility brings a man honor; his courage sustains his broken body. Intelligent people are open to new ideas and actively look for them. A wife is a blessing from the Lord, and the man who finds her finds a good thing. A real friend is closer than a brother.

Chapter 18
Key Points: Things to Seek, Be, or Do

1. Be wise so that your words express deep streams of thought.
2. The Lord is a strong fortress; be godly and run to him and be safe.
3. Your humility ends in honor.
4. Your courage can sustain your broken body.
5. Be intelligent and open to new ideas and look for them.
6. A bribe does wonders; it brings you before men of importance.
7. Use a coin toss to end arguments against powerful opponents.
8. Wise advice will satisfy you like a good meal.
9. If you find a wife, you have found a good thing; she is a blessing from the Lord.
10. It's better to be the poor man who pleads, than the rich man who insults.
11. Some of your friends are closer than brothers.

CHAPTER 18

What God Wants Us to Avoid

Chapter 18 mentions the negative traits of the rebel who ignores all facts and yells. This selfish man breaks the code of conduct, quarrels, and demands his own way. This fool fights constantly and runs his mouth until words become his undoing and his sin brings disgrace. Some love to talk, so they suffer the consequences and die from saying the wrong thing. Rumors are dainty morsels eaten with great relish, but how stupid and shameful to decide before knowing the facts? Any story sounds true until the other side is told and sets the record straight. It is wrong for a judge to favor the wicked and condemn the innocent. The rich man thinks his wealth is an impenetrable high wall of defense; what a dreamer! His insults hurt him, and his pride ends in destruction. When courage dies, what hope is left, for the lazy man is brother to the saboteur. Some are friends in name only, but it is harder to win back the friendship of an offended brother than capture a fortified city.

Chapter 18
Key Points: Things to Avoid

1. Don't be a selfish person who quarrels, breaks the code of conduct, and demands your own way.
2. Don't be a rebel who doesn't care about facts but only yells.
3. Your sin brings disgrace.
4. It is wrong for a judge to favor you if you are wicked and condemn you if you are innocent.
5. Don't be a fool who gets into constant fights; your mouth will be your undoing. Your words endanger you.
6. Rumors are dainty morsels; you eat them with great relish!
7. Being a lazy person is being the brother of the saboteur.
8. As a rich person, you will think your wealth is an impregnable high wall of defense. What a dreamer!
9. Your pride ends in destruction.
10. Don't be stupid because deciding before knowing the facts is a shame.
11. When your courage dies, what hope is left?
12. Any story sounds to you true until the other side is told and straightens the record.
13. It's harder for you to win back the friendship of an offended brother than capture a fortified city; their anger shuts you out like iron bars.
14. If you love to talk, then suffer the consequences; men die for saying the wrong thing.
15. Don't be a rich person who answers with insults.
16. Some people are your friends in name only.

CHAPTER 19

Things to Seek, Be, or Do

In Chapter 19, the godly see it's better to be poor and honest than the opposite; a poor man has no unneeded friends, but if he is generous, he will have many friends. Those who help the poor lend to the Lord, and what a tremendous interest on the loan! He who loves wisdom is successful because he loves his best interest. To his credit, the wise man restrains his anger and overlooks insults. They should keep the commandments and keep their life, for false witnesses are punished, and liars tracked down. A king's approval is refreshing as dew on the grass. While a father can give a son homes and riches, only the Lord can provide an understanding wife. They should discipline a son early in life while there is hope. Finally, individuals need all the advice they can get and be wise for the rest of their lives.

Chapter 19
Key Points: Things to Seek, Be, or Do

1. It is better for you to be poor and honest than the opposite.
2. If you are poor, you will have no friends left.
3. Punish false witnesses and track down liars.
4. If you are generous, many people will beg from you, and you'll have many friends.
5. If you love wisdom, you love your own best interest and will be a success.
6. Be wise and restrain anger and overlook insults; this is to your credit.
7. Be as refreshing as the dew on the grass and win the king's approval.
8. As a father, you can give your son homes and riches.
9. Keep the commandments and keep your life.
10. Help the poor, and you lend to the Lord (with a beautiful interest on the loan!)
11. Discipline your son early in life while there is hope.
12. Get all the advice you can and be wise for the rest of your life.
13. You are an attractive man if you are kind.
14. Have reverence for God, which gives life, happiness, and protection from harm.
15. Punish a mocker, and others will learn from it.
16. Reprove a wise man, and he will become wiser.

CHAPTER 19

What God Wants Us to Avoid

Chapter 19 explains it is sinful and dangerous to rush into the unknown. Many would rather be dishonest and rich. The wealthy man has "friends" but ruins his chances with his own foolishness and then blames the Lord. The liar will be caught and the false witness punished. This poor man's own brothers turn from him in embarrassment; how much more his friends! He calls for them, but they are gone. It's wrong for a fool to succeed or a slave to rule over a prince. When this happens, the king's anger is as dangerous as a lion's. A rebellious son is a calamity to his father, and a lack of discipline will ruin his life, for despising the commandments means death. For man proposes, but God disposes. A lazy man sleeps and goes hungry. Some men are so lazy they won't even feed themselves. A nagging wife annoys like dripping, and a short-tempered man must bear his own penalty, and you can't help him. If you try once, you must try a dozen times. A son who mistreats his mother and father is a public disgrace. A worthless witness cares nothing for the truth and enjoys his sinning too much. He should stop listening to teaching that contradicts what they know is right. It is better to be poor than dishonest, and mockers and rebels will be severely punished.

Chapter 19
Key Points: Things to Avoid

1. Avoid being both dishonest and rich.
2. It is dangerous and sinful for you to rush into the unknown.
3. You will ruin your chances by your own foolishness and then blame the Lord.
4. If you are wealthy, you will have many "friends."
5. Don't be a liar or a false witness.
6. If you are poor, your own brothers turn from you in embarrassment; how much more your friends! (You call for them, but they are gone.)
7. Be a false witness and you shall be punished; be a liar and you will perish.
8. If you're a fool, it's wrong for you to succeed or, if you are a slave, to rule over a prince.
9. Don't provoke the king's anger; it is as dangerous as a lion's.
10. If you are a rebellious son, you are a calamity to your father.
11. Don't be a nagging wife who annoys like dripping.
12. Only the Lord can give your son an understanding wife.
13. Don't be lazy or you'll sleep and go hungry.
14. If you despise commandments, it means death.
15. Don't be a son who has no discipline or you will ruin your life.
16. The short-tempered man must bear his own penalty; you can't help him. If you try once, you must try a dozen times.
17. You propose, but God disposes.
18. It's better for you to be poor than dishonest.
19. Don't be like some who are so lazy that they won't even feed themselves.
20. Don't be a son who mistreats his father or mother; you will be a public disgrace.
21. Stop listening to teaching that contradicts what you know is right.
22. Don't be a worthless witness who cares nothing for truth and enjoys sinning too much.
23. Don't be mockers or rebels; they will be severely punished.

CHAPTER 20

Things to Seek, Be, or Do

Chapter 20 is an interactive mix of humanity, God, old, young, truth, and punishment. Specifically, the wise man draws good advice deep from within a counselor's heart. It is an honor to stay out of a fight. We can even know a child's character by how he or she acts and if what that child does is pure and right. It is a wonderful heritage to have an honest father to guide us during these times. Those who have good eyesight and good hearing should thank God who gave these gifts to them. Persons should stay awake, work hard, and there will be plenty to eat. A king who acts as a judge weighs all evidence carefully, distinguishing what is true and what is false, as good sense is far more valuable than precious jewels, and if a king is kind, honest, and fair, his kingdom stands secure. A man's conscience is the Lord's searchlight, exposing his hidden motives. A wise man stamps out crime with severe punishment, and the penalty must hurt; it chases evil from the heart. The glory of young men is their strength, of older men, their experience. Since the Lord directs individuals' steps, why should they try to understand everything that happens along the way?

Chapter 20
Key Points: Things to Seek, Be, or Do

1. It is an honor for you to stay out of a fight.
2. Good advice lies deep within a counselor's heart; be a wise man and draw it out.
3. You have a wonderful heritage if you have an honest father.
4. A king who acts as a judge weighs all evidence carefully, distinguishing what is true and false.
5. Be sure your child behaves; his character is known by how he acts and if it is pure and right.
6. If you have good eyesight and hearing, thank God who gave them to you.
7. Stay awake, work hard, and there will be plenty to eat.
8. You must recognize God's sense as far more valuable than precious jewels.
9. Since the Lord directs your steps, why try to understand everything that happens along the way?
10. Be a wise man who stamps out crime with severe punishment.
11. Your conscience is the Lord's searchlight, exposing your hidden motives.
12. Encourage the king to be kind, honest, and fair, and his kingdom will stand secure.
13. When young, your glory is your strength; when older you have your experience.
14. Punishment that hurts you chases evil from the heart.

CHAPTER 20

What God Wants Us to Avoid

Chapter 20 explores cheating, drinking, and a host of sins. Specifically, only fools insist on quarreling, given false courage from liquor and wine that leads to brawls. What fools these men are to let alcohol master them, making them stagger drunkenly down the street. They are lazy and won't eat in the harvest if they don't plow in the cold. And if they love to sleep, they will live in poverty. Fools are on the wrong path; they tell themselves that they have loyal friends but are they being told the truth? For it is risky to make a loan to a stranger. And who can ever say, "I have cleansed my heart; I am sinless." The king's fury is like a roaring lion; to rouse his anger is to risk their life. The Lord despises every kind of cheating. He loathes all dishonesty. "Utterly worthless," says the buyer, haggling over price, but he brags about the bargain afterward. They can make a fortune from cheating, but a curse goes with it. Some enjoy cheating, but the cake they receive from ill-gotten gain will become gravel in their mouths. Something to remember: They shouldn't tell their secrets to a gossiper unless they want them broadcasted to the world. God puts out the light of the man who curses his father or mother. They shouldn't repay evil for evil; wait for the Lord to handle it. It is foolish and rash to make a promise to the Lord before counting the cost.

Chapter 21
Key Points: Things to Seek, Be, or Do

1. Be like the king whose thoughts are directed by the Lord like water into irrigation ditches.
2. God is more pleased when you are just and fair than when you give him gifts.
3. Steady plodding brings you prosperity.
4. You are known for your actions; if you are good, you live a godly life.
5. It is better for you to live in the corner attic with a good woman than with a crabby woman in a lovely home.
6. If you are wise, you will learn by listening.
7. The godly learn by watching ruin overtake the wicked.
8. The good man loves justice.
9. The righteous will finally win.
10. It is better to live in the desert than to live in a home with a quarrelsome woman.
11. If you are wise, you will save for the future.
12. If you try to be good, loving, and kind, you will find life, righteousness, and honor.
13. Be wise and you will conquer the strong man and level his defense.
14. Keep your mouth closed, and you will stay out of trouble.
15. If you have godly love, you will give.
16. If you are an honest witness, you will be safe.
17. You will show that you are godly when you reconsider the situation.
18. Go ahead and prepare for the conflict, but victory comes from God.

CHAPTER 21

What God Wants Us to Avoid

Chapter 21 shows that they can justify every deed, but God sees their motives. The dishonest gain will never last, so why take the risk? A man is known for his actions, and an evil man lives a wicked life. His pride, lust, and evil actions are all sins. Because the wicked are unfair, their violence boomerangs and destroys them. Their hasty speculation brings poverty. Even if they have a lovely home, they will share it with a crabby and quarrelsome woman. The evil man loves to harm others, and being a good neighbor is out of the question. The simpleton only learns by seeing scorners punished. He shuts his ears to the cries of the poor so that they will ignore him during his own time of need. The foolish man spends whatever he gets, and the angry man is silenced when given a gift. The lazy man is greedy and longs for many things but refuses to work. God loathes the gifts of all evil men, especially if they try to bribe him. The wicked will finally lose, for justice is a calamity to evildoers. The man who loves pleasure ends up poor, as wine and luxury are not the way to riches. A false witness must be punished, and the evil man is stubborn. These mockers are proud, haughty, and arrogant; they stray from common sense and end up dead. No one, no matter how shrewd or well-advised can stand against the Lord.

Chapter 21
Key Points: Things to Avoid

1. You can justify every deed, but God directs your motives.
2. Your pride, lust, and evil actions are all sins.
3. Your dishonest gain will never last, so why take the risk?
4. If you have hasty speculation, it will bring poverty.
5. Being wicked means being unfair; your violence boomerangs and destroys you.
6. You are known for your actions; an evil person lives an evil life.
7. It is far worse for you to live with a crabby woman in a lovely home than in the attic with a good woman.
8. Don't be an evil person who loves to harm others and finds being a good neighbor is out of line.
9. If you are a simpleton, you only learn by seeing scorners punished.
10. If you shut your ears to the cries of the poor, you will be ignored during your own time of need.
11. Silence an angry man by giving him a gift.
12. You will see that justice is a calamity to evildoers.
13. Don't stray away from common sense or you'll end up dead.
14. If you love pleasure, you will end up poor; wine and luxury are not the way to riches.
15. Don't be wicked, for they will finally lose.
16. It's hard for you to live with the quarrelsome, complaining woman.
17. Don't be foolish and spend whatever you get.
18. Don't be mockers who are proud, haughty, and arrogant.
19. If you are lazy, you will long for many things but refuse to work to get them.
20. Don't be like evil men whose gifts God loathes, especially if they try to bribe him.
21. If you are a false witness, you must be punished.
22. If you are evil, you are stubborn.
23. No one, including you, no matter how shrewd or well-advised, can stand against the Lord.

CHAPTER 22

Things to Seek, Be, or Do

Chapter 22 explores more basic living skills and advice. More specifically, if they must choose, choose a good name and loving esteem over the riches of silver and gold. The rich and poor are alike before the Lord because he made them all. The prudent man sees difficulties ahead and prepares for them. He values his soul and stays away from the wrong road. He teaches his child to choose the right path so that he will remain upon it when he is older. He uses discipline and punishment to drive rebellion from his child. True humility and respect for the Lord lead a man to riches, honor, and long life. This is the happy and generous man who feeds the poor. Do they know a hardworking man? He shall be successful and stand before kings. He who values grace and truth is the king's friend. They should throw out the mocker, and they will be rid of tension, fighting, and quarrels, for the Lord preserves the upright. He must listen to wise advice; it will do him good. He must pass it on to others. He must trust in the Lord and share this with the people.

Chapter 22
Key Points: Things to Seek, Be, or Do

1. Take a good man over promising riches.
2. Take loving esteem over silver and gold.
3. Whether you are rich or poor, you are alike before the Lord because he made you all.
4. Be prudent and see difficulties and plan for them.
5. True humility and respect for the Lord lead you to riches, honor, and long life.
6. Value your soul and stay away from the treacherous road.
7. Teach a child to choose the right path; when older, he will remain upon it.
8. You will be happy if you are generous and feed the poor.
9. Throw out the mocker, and you will be rid of tension, fighting, and quarrels.
10. You will be the king's friend if you value grace and truth.
11. Be upright and the Lord will preserve you.
12. You should use punishment to drive rebellion out of the youngster.
13. Listen to wise advice; it will do you good.
14. Pass wise advice to others.
15. Trust in the Lord; he's been right in the past, so believe me now and share him with others.
16. Do you know a hardworking man? He shall be successful and stand before kings.

CHAPTER 22

What God Wants Us to Avoid

Chapter 22 discusses rebels and their mistakes. The simpleton chooses silver, gold, and riches over a good name, yet he blindly pushes on, suffers the consequences, and walks a thorny, treacherous road. The Lord ruins the plans of the wicked. The lazy man is full of excuses: "I can't go to work; I might meet a lion and be killed!" Just as the rich rule the poor, the borrower is a servant to the lender, and unless someone has extra cash on hand, he shouldn't countersign the note. Why risk everything he owns? They'll even take his bed. The youngster's heart is full of rebellion. The prostitute is a dangerous trap to him, and those cursed by God are caught in it. The unjust tyrant will reap disaster, and his reign of terror will end. He who gains by oppressing the poor or bribing the rich will end in poverty. No one should rob the poor and sick, for the Lord is their defender, and he will punish anyone who injures them. Angry, short-tempered men must be avoided because those who learn from them will endanger their souls. Finally, moving the ancient boundary markers is stealing.

Chapter 22
Key Points: Things to Avoid

1. Don't be like the simpleton who prefers riches, silver, and gold over a good name and loving esteem.
2. Don't be like the simpleton who does not plan ahead and suffers the consequences.
3. Don't be a rebel who walks the thorny, treacherous road.
4. Pay attention: As the rich rule the poor, the borrower is a servant to the lender.
5. Don't be the unjust tyrant; otherwise, you will find disaster, and your reign of terror will end.
6. Don't be wicked or the Lord will ruin your plans.
7. Don't be lazy and full of excuses: "I can't go to work; I might meet a lion and be killed."
8. You will find that a prostitute is a dangerous trap; those cursed by God are caught in it.
9. When you are a youngster, your heart is full of rebellion.
10. If you gain by oppressing the poor or bribing the rich, you will end in poverty.
11. Don't rob the poor and sick. The Lord is their defender; if you injure them, he will punish you.
12. Keep away from angry, short-tempered men, lest you learn from them and endanger your soul.
13. Unless you have extra cash, don't countersign any note. Why risk everything you own? They'll even take your bed.
14. Don't move the ancient boundary markers. That is stealing.

CHAPTER 23

Things to Seek, Be, or Do

Chapter 23 continues with good family advice. Specifically, God will rejoice in those who become people of common sense. Others' hearts will be thrilled by thoughtful, wise words. Individuals must have reverence for the Lord always, and they will have a fantastic future ahead. It will show there is hope for them yet! They are wise and stay on God's path. They get the facts at any price and hold on to all the good sense they can get. They correct their children, knowing discipline is helpful and won't hurt them. Children won't die if a stick is used on them; punishment keeps them out of hell. Children must listen to their father's wise advice and not despise a mother's experience. Godly individuals will accept criticism and get all the help they can get. The father of the godly man has cause for joy. What pleasure a wise son is; he gives his parents great joy!

Chapter 23
Key Points: Things to Seek, Be, or Do

1. Correct your children, discipline won't hurt them; they won't die if you use a stick on them.
2. Punishing your children keeps them out of hell.
3. Accept criticism and get all the help you can.
4. The Lord will rejoice if you become a man of common sense. His heart will thrill with your thoughtful, wise words.
5. Have reverence for the Lord all the time, for indeed you have a fantastic future ahead. There is hope for you yet!
6. Be wise and stay on God's path.
7. Listen to your father's advice and don't despise an old mother's experience.
8. Get the facts at any price and hold onto all the good sense you can get.
9. If you are godly, your father has cause for joy.
10. What a pleasure a wise son is. Sons, give your parents joy.

CHAPTER 23

What God Wants Us to Avoid

In Chapter 23, we are taught about the dangers of stealing and using alcohol, among others things. Specifically, people must not steal the land of defenseless orphans by moving boundary markers, for the strong redeemer will accuse them himself. People should not envy evil men or carouse with drunkards and gluttons, for they are on their way to poverty. Their extra sleep clothes them in rags. Likewise, wise men stay away from prostitutes; they dig a deep and narrow grave for their victims, as one after another are unfaithful to their wives. Are individuals' hearts filled with anguish and sorrow? Are they constantly fighting and quarreling? Do they have bloodshot eyes, many wounds, or long hours trying out new tavern mixtures? They shouldn't be deceived by the sparkle and smooth taste of intense wine. Alcohol will cause hallucinations and delirium tremens. Those under the influence will say foolish, silly things that would be embarrassing if they were sober. They will stagger as a drunken sailor tossed at sea, clinging to a swaying mast. And they will say, "I didn't even know it when they beat me up; let's go and have another drink!" In the end, alcohol bites like a poisonous serpent and stings like a viper.

Chapter 24
Key Points: Things to Seek, Be, or Do

1. Your wise planning builds an enterprise, which becomes strong through common sense and profits by using facts.
2. Be wise and you will be mightier than the strong man, for wisdom is mightier than strength.
3. There's safety in many counselors; don't go to war without wise guidance.
4. Rescue those unjustly sentenced to death:

   A. Don't stand back and let them die.
   B. Don't say you didn't know, for God who knows all hearts knows yours. And he knows you knew!
   C. He will reward you according to your deeds!

5. Honey and wisdom whet your appetite.
6. When you enjoy wisdom, there is hope for you. A bright future lies ahead.
7. You may trip the upright man seven times, but he will rise each time.
8. Blessings shower you if you rebuke sin fearlessly.
9. It's an honor for you to receive a frank reply.
10. Develop your business before you build your home.
11. Watch your step before the Lord and King.

CHAPTER 24

What God Wants Us to Avoid

Chapter 24 warns people of the wayward ways of those on the wrong road. Specifically, they should avoid envying the godless men and their company, those who spend their days plotting violence and cheating. Planning evil is as bad as doing it. These rebels despise wisdom, won't be chosen as a counselor, and fail to choose wise advice from wise men. The rebel's schemes are sinful, and the mocker is the scourge of all humankind. Wise men watch their step before the Lord and King and don't associate with radicals, for they'll go down with the radicals to sudden disaster. The strong man is weaker than the wise man, so it's best to avoid war without guidance and wise counselors, for who knows where it will end up. A person is a poor specimen if he can't stand pressure and adversity. To the evil man, leave the upright man alone and quit trying to cheat him out of his rights, for though the evil man may trip him seven times; he will rise each time, while the evil man will stumble when calamity strikes. And it's wrong to sentence the poor and let the rich go free. Moreover, if someone calls the wicked "innocent," that individual will be cursed by many nations. If someone testifies and lies about an innocent neighbor, he shouldn't be paid back for meanness; let the Lord handle it. When an enemy meets trouble, the wise man won't rejoice. There should be no gladness when he falls, for the Lord may become displeased and stop punishing him. The wicked should not be envied, nor should their riches be coveted. The evil man has no future; his light will be snuffed out. The field of a lazy man has thorns, weeds, and broken walls. It teaches a valuable lesson: extra sleep, more slumber, and folding one's hands behind his head to rest leads to poverty. And it happens suddenly, like a robber, and violently, like a bandit.

Chapter 24
Key Points: Things to Avoid

1. Don't envy godless men or their company, for they spend their day plotting violence and evil.
2. Be wise because the strong man is weaker than the wise man; strength is weaker than wisdom.
3. Don't be like the rebel who rushes into war without counsel.
4. Don't be like the rebels who despise wisdom; they won't be chosen as counselors.
5. Don't plan evil, which is as wrong as doing it.
6. Avoid the rebel's schemes, which are sinful; the mocker is the scourge of all mankind.
7. You are a poor specimen if you can't stand the pressure of adversity.
8. Evil men leave the upright man alone; quit trying to cheat him out of his rights.
9. Be warned that one calamity is enough to lay the evil man low.
10. Don't rejoice when your enemy meets trouble; let there be no gladness when he falls, for the Lord may become displeased with you and stop punishing him.
11. Don't envy the wicked or covet his riches.
12. The evil man has no future; his light will be snuffed out.
13. Avoid associating with radicals, or you'll go down with them to sudden disaster, and who knows where it will end.
14. Don't sentence the poor and let the rich go free.
15. If you call the wicked "innocent," you'll be cursed by many nations.
16. Don't testify and lie about an innocent neighbor; don't pay him back for meanness.
17. Don't be lazy; the lazy man's field has thorns, weeds, and broken walls.
18. Extra sleep, more slumber, and folding your hands to rest leads to poverty, and it comes suddenly like a robber and violently like a bandit.

CHAPTER 25

Things to Seek, Be, or Do

Chapter 25 reveals that the Proverbs of Solomon were found and copied by the aides of King Hezekiah from Judah. It is God's privilege to conceal, for mankind can't understand heaven's height or earth's size. No one knows what happens in the king's mind, who has the privilege to discover and invent. Like removing the impurities from silver to get sterling, God instructs that they remove all corrupt men from the king's court, so his reign will be just and fair. They should welcome those who give timely advice, which is as lovely as golden apples in a silver basket. They should accept criticism, which is a badge of honor. They should be patient, and they'll finally win by remembering that a soft tongue can break hard bones. A faithful employee is as refreshing as a cool day during a hot summer. The good news from far away is like cold water to those thirsty. If an enemy is hungry, one should give them food. If they are thirsty, one should give them something to drink. This generosity shames them, and God will reward the giver.

Chapter 25
Key Points: Things to Seek, Be, or Do

1. Search the Scriptures like the aides of the king of Hezekiah, who found and copied the Proverbs of Solomon.
2. Ponder this: God's privilege is to conceal, and the king's privilege is to discover and invent.
3. When you remove the trash from silver, you get sterling.
4. When you remove corrupt men from the king's court, his reign will be just and fair.
5. The timely advice you receive is as lovely as golden apples in a silver basket.
6. It is a badge of honor for you to accept valid criticism.
7. Be a faithful employee who is as refreshing as a cool day in the hot summertime.
8. Be patient, and you'll finally win, for a soft tongue can break hard bones.
9. If your enemies are hungry, give them food; if thirsty, give them a drink. They will be ashamed of themselves, and God will reward you.
10. If you receive good news from far away, it is like cold water to the thirsty.

CHAPTER 25

What God Wants Us to Avoid

Chapter 25 expounds on more character traits to avoid. Specifically, one should wait for an invitation from the king. One shouldn't act like a mighty prince, demanding an audience with him and possibly becoming a public disgrace. One shouldn't be a hothead and rush to court for a shameful defeat. Instead, one should discuss the matter privately without telling anyone else in order to avoid being accused of slander. Those who don't deliver the promised gifts are like the cloud refusing to drop cool rain over a hot desert. It is harmful to a man to be sitting around overeating honey and thinking about the honors he deserves; besides, overeating honey will make him sick. A man without self-control is as defenseless as the broken walls of a city. He will wear out his welcome if he visits his neighbor too often. Lying about someone is like stabbing them with an axe, sword, or arrow. Being happy around someone with a broken heart is like rubbing salt in their wounds or stealing their jacket in cold weather. Like the north wind brings cold, a poor reply causes anger. Living in the corner of an attic is better than in a beautiful home with a quarrelsome woman. Putting confidence in an unreliable man is like chewing with a sore tooth or running on a broken foot. And the godly man who compromises with the wicked is like polluting a freshwater fountain or muddying up a spring.

Chapter 25
Key Points: Things to Avoid

1. You can't understand the height of heaven, the size of earth, or what goes on in the king's mind.

2. Don't demand an audience with the king as if you were a mighty prince; wait for an invitation, or you will be publicly disgraced.

3. Don't be a hothead and rush to court, or it could mean shameful defeat. Instead, discuss the matter privately. Don't tell anyone lest they accuse you of slander.

4. If you don't give a gift you promised, it is like a cloud over a desert without dropping any rain.

5. Don't overeat honey; it will make you sick.

6. Don't visit your neighbor too often, or you'll wear out your welcome!

7. Your telling lies about someone is as harmful as wounding them with an axe, sword, or sharp arrow.

8. Don't put confidence in an unreliable man; it is like chewing with a sore tooth or running on a broken foot.

9. Don't be happy-go-lucky around someone with a broken heart. It is like stealing their jacket in cold weather or rubbing salt in their wounds.

10. Like the north wind brings cold, giving a sharp retort causes anger.

11. It's better for you to live in a corner attic than in a beautiful home with a quarrelsome woman.

12. If you are godly but compromise with the wicked, it is like polluting a fountain or muddying a spring.

13. Overeating honey and thinking about all the honors you deserve is harmful.

14. If you have no self-control, you are as defenseless as a city's broken-down walls.

CHAPTER 26

Things to Seek, Be, or Do

Chapter 26 reveals more steps to keeping the peace in one's life to honor God. Specifically, like a sparrow or swallow flying by, no harm comes to one who receives an undeserved curse. It will not affect him. Therefore, the master may get better help from an untrained apprentice than from a skilled rebel. While the horse is guided with a whip and a donkey with a bridle, guide the rebel with a rod to his back. As the fire goes out when there is a lack of fuel, so does all tension when gossip stops.

Chapter 26
Key Points: Things to Seek, Be, or Do

1. An undeserved curse has no effect on and produces no harm to you, like a flying sparrow or swallow.
2. While the horse is guided with a whip and a donkey with a bridle, if you are a rebel, you'll be guided with a rod to your back.
3. As a master, you may get better help from an untrained apprentice than a skilled rebel.
4. Fire goes out when there is no fuel as tensions disappear when your gossip stops.

CHAPTER 26

What God Wants Us to Avoid

Chapter 26 explains the many perils of the rebel. Specifically, honors go to fools like snow in the summertime or rain during the harvest. And like a stone in a slingshot, honoring the rebel will backfire. Therefore, one shouldn't argue with a fool or get into foolish arguments, which cause him to look equally ridiculous. Instead, he should prick the fool's conceit with silly replies, for the quarrelsome man starts a fight as quickly as paper being set on fire with a match. And it's no more foolish to yank on a dog's ears than to interfere in an argument that's not one's business. Trusting a rebel to share a message is like cutting off one's feet and drinking poison. A proverb in the mouth of a fool is like a paralyzed leg. A rebel will misuse an illustration to make a point, but like a thorn in the hand of a drunkard, one will not feel it. And so, as a dog returns to his vomit, a fool returns to repeat his folly. But, of course, one thing worse than a fool is the arrogant man. The lazy man won't go outside to work: "There might be a lion!" So instead, he sticks to his bed like hinges to a door. He's too tired to lift food to his mouth, yet he claims his opinion is more intelligent than seven wise men. Gossip is a dainty morsel eaten with great relish. But a man caught lying and saying he was "fooling" is like a mad man throwing arrows and smoldering cinders to create strife and death. So don't be fooled; lovely words may hide a wicked heart like a pretty glaze on a standard pot. The man with hate sounds pleasant, but they shouldn't believe him. He curses them in his heart. His flattery is a form of hatred that wounds cruelly. He pretends to be kind, but his hatred will finally be known for all to see. If a man rolls a boulder on someone, it will roll back and crush the person. Likewise, the man who sets a trap for others will get caught himself.

Chapter 26
Key Points: Things to Avoid

1. Don't be the fool whose honors are like snow in the summertime or rain in the harvest.
2. Don't be a rebel who always needs a rod to his back.
3. Are you arguing with a fool? Don't use foolish arguments, or you will look ridiculous. Instead, prick his conceit with silly replies.
4. Trusting a rebel to share a message is like cutting off your feet and drinking poison.
5. Don't be a fool. In the mouth of a fool, a proverb is like a paralyzed leg.
6. If you honor a rebel, it will backfire like a stone in a slingshot.
7. A rebel will misuse an illustration to make a point. Like a thorn in the hand of a drunkard, you will not feel it.
8. As a dog returns to vomit, if you are a fool, you will return to repeat your folly.
9. One thing worse than your being a fool is being an arrogant man.
10. Don't be a lazy man won't go to work outside because "There might be a lion!"
11. If you are a lazy man, you will stick to your bed like a door to its hinges!
12. Don't be a lazy man who is too tired to lift his food to his mouth.
13. Don't be the lazy man who claims his opinion is more intelligent than seven wise men.
14. Yanking a dog's ears is no more foolish than interfering in an argument that isn't your business.
15. Don't be caught lying and saying you were "fooling." It's like a madman throwing firebrands, arrows, and death.
16. If you are quarrelsome, you start fights as quickly as a match sets fire to paper.
17. Your gossip is a dainty morsel eaten with great relish.

18. Beware. Your pretty words may hide a wicked heart like a pretty glaze on a standard clay pot.
19. A man with hate in his heart may sound pleasant, but don't believe him, for he curses you in his heart.
20. The man with hate pretends to be kind, but his hatred will finally become known for you and everyone else to see.
21. If you set a trap for others, you will yourself get caught. If you roll a boulder on someone, it will roll back and crush you.
22. Your flattery is a form of hatred and cruelly wounds.

CHAPTER 27

Things to Seek, Be, or Do

Chapter 27 reveals more common-sense measures to live the good life. Specifically, one should be humble about future plans and see what tomorrow brings. He should let others praise him, for while the purity of silver and gold is tested in a crucible, a man is tested by his reaction to praise. Finally, he must accept criticism because an open rebuke is better than hidden love, and wounds from a friend are better than kisses from an enemy. He should never abandon a friend, either his own or his father's, and then he won't need to go to a distant relative for help. Friendly suggestions are as pleasant as perfume. An excellent discussion is as stimulating as the sparks that fly when iron strikes iron. Who a man is comes not in a reflection in a mirror but is shown by the kind of friends he chooses. How happy a father will be if the son turns out to be sensible, for it brings him public honor. The sensible man watches for problems ahead and prepares. A worker should be able to eat from any orchard he takes care of, so one should reward anyone who protects another person's interest, but he should watch his business, or his money will disappear fast. Even the king's crown and riches don't stay in his family forever. One should know his flocks and herds; then he'll have sheep's wool for clothing and goat's milk for food. If he works hard, the new crops will appear after harvesting hay and gathering grass.

Chapter 27
Key Points: Things to Seek, Be, or Do

1. Wait and see what plans God has in store for you.
2. Let others praise you.
3. Your being given an open rebuke is better than hidden love.
4. Wounds from your friend are better than kisses from your enemy.
5. Friendly suggestions given to you are as pleasant as perfume.
6. Never abandon a friend, either yours or your father's. Then you won't need to go to a distant relative.
7. How happy I will be, son, if you turn out to be sensible. It will be a public honor for me.
8. If you are sensible, you will watch for problems ahead and prepare.
9. Have a friendly discussion, which is as stimulating as the sparks that fly when iron strikes iron.
10. A worker should be able to eat food from the orchard he tends. Reward anyone who protects another person's interest.
11. A mirror reflects your face, but what you are really like is shown by the kind of friends you choose.
12. The purity of silver and gold is tested in a crucible, but you are tested by your reaction to praise.
13. Watch your business. Riches disappear fast, and even the king's crown doesn't stay in his family forever. Know your flocks and herds.
14. Watching your business means you'll have wool for clothing and goat's milk for food. Then, after the hay is harvested, grasses are gathered, and the new crop appears.

CHAPTER 27

What God Wants Us to Avoid

Chapter 27 expounds on a variety of negative points to avoid. Specifically, one shouldn't brag about his plans when God determines what comes together. He should avoid praising himself. A rebel's frustration is heavier than sand and rocks. His jealousy is more dangerous and crueler than anger. Even honey seems tasteless to a full man, but if he is hungry, he'll eat anything! A man who strays away from his home is like a bird that wanders from his nest. The man who agrees to pay a stranger's debts is the world's poorest credit risk. Even shooting a pleasant greeting to a friend too early in the morning will be counted as a curse. A cranky woman and the annoying dripping on a rainy day are the same. A man can't stop her any more than he can control the wind from blowing. It's like trying to hold something with oily or slippery hands. Both ambition and death are alike in that neither is satisfied. A man can crush a rebel into powder, but he can't separate him from his foolishness.

Chapter 27
Key Points: Things to Avoid

1. Don't brag about your plans.
2. Avoid praising yourself.
3. Don't be a rebel whose frustrations are heavier than sand and rocks.
4. Your jealousy is more dangerous and crueler than anger.
5. Even honey seems tasteless if you are full, but if hungry, you'll eat anything!
6. If you stray from your home, you are like a bird that wanders from its nest.
7. Don't be a simpleton who never looks ahead and suffers the consequences.
8. You are the world's poorest credit risk if you agree to pay a stranger's debts.
9. If you shout a pleasant greeting to a friend too early in the morning, it will be counted as a curse.
10. A cranky woman and dripping on a rainy day are the same.
11. You can't stop her complaints any more than you can stop the wind or use oily hands to hold onto something.
12. Beware. Your ambition and deceit are alike in that neither is ever satisfied.
13. You can crush a rebel into powder, but you can't separate him from his foolishness.

CHAPTER 28

Things to Seek, Be, or Do

Chapter 28 depicts more ways to improve life and become more successful. Specifically, the godly are as bold as lions. In addition, there is government stability where there are honest leaders, for those who obey the law fight evil. These people who follow the Lord care about justice. They know it's better to be poor and honest than rich and a liar. Therefore, young men who obey the law are wise. Men who encourage the upright to do good will be given a worthy award. When the godly are successful, everyone is glad. If he confesses his mistakes and forsakes them, he gets another chance. For blessed is the man who reveres God. Even the king who hates dishonesty and bribes will have a long reign. People appreciate frankness over flattery. Good men will be rescued from harm. Their hard work brings prosperity, and the man who wants to do the right thing is given a rich award. Trusting God leads to prosperity, and those who use God's wisdom are safe. If you give to the poor, God will supply all of a person's needs. And when the wicked meet disaster, good men will take over and lead.

Chapter 28
Key Points: Things to Seek, Be, or Do

1. If you are godly, you are as bold as a lion.
2. There is stability if you have honest and sensible leaders.
3. Obey the law, for doing so fights evil.
4. If you follow the Lord, you care about justice.
5. It is better for you to be poor and honest than the opposite.
6. Young men who obey the law are wise.
7. Be the men who encourage the upright, and you will be given a worthwhile award.
8. When you are godly and successful, everyone is glad.
9. If you confess your mistakes, you get another chance.
10. Blessed is the man who reveres God.
11. A king who hates dishonesty and bribes will have a long reign.
12. If you are good, you will be rescued from harm.
13. Your hard work brings prosperity.
14. If you want to do the right thing, you will get a rich award.
15. People appreciate your frankness over flattery.
16. Trust God, which leads to prosperity.
17. You will be safe if you use God's wisdom.
18. If you give to the poor, God supplies your needs.
19. When the wicked meet disaster, good men will return to lead.

CHAPTER 28

What God Wants Us to Avoid

Chapter 28 covers many negative traits of the wicked who flee when no one is chasing them. Specifically, the government of moral rot is toppled easily within a nation, and complaining about the law is praising wickedness. When a poor man oppresses an even poorer man, it's like the unexpected flood sweeping away their last hope. Money from exploiting the poor will end up in the hands of those who pity them. Evil men don't understand the importance of justice; they would rather cheat and be rich. When a son belongs to a lawless gang, it brings shame to his father. God doesn't listen to the prayers of those who flout the law. And there is a curse on those who lead the godly astray. The man who rejects God and refuses to admit his mistakes is headed for trouble, so he can never be successful. And when the wicked succeed, everyone is sad. These rich men are arrogant, and their "real poverty" is evident to the poor. The wicked man is as dangerous to the poor as the bear attack or a lion's mauling. And only a stupid king would oppress his people. A murderer's conscience will drive him into hell, so don't stop him. Those who cheat will be destroyed; poverty comes to those who play around and won't work. Even those who use get-rich-quick schemes will quickly fail. Trying to get rich quick is evil and leads to poverty. Greed causes fighting, and giving preferred treatment to the rich is like selling one's soul for a piece of bread. Don't be like the man who robs his parents and says, "What's wrong with that?" He is no better than a murderer. A fool is a man who trusts himself and receives a curse for closing his eyes to poverty. For when the wicked prosper, good men go away.

Chapter 28
Key Points: Things to Avoid

1. Don't be wicked, or you will flee when no one is watching you.
2. If you have moral rot within the nation, the government topples easily.
3. Watch out for a poor man who oppresses a poorer man. It's like an unexpected flood sweeping away their last hope.
4. Don't be evil or you won't understand the importance of justice.
5. It's worse for you to cheat and be rich than the opposite.
6. If you are a son who belongs to a lawless gang, you are a shame to your father.
7. If you gain money from exploiting the poor, it will end up in the hands of those who pity them.
8. God doesn't listen to your prayers if you flout the law.
9. Don't be cursed by leading the godly astray.
10. Don't be the arrogant rich man whose "real poverty" is evident to the poor.
11. Don't be the wicked person who creates sadness when you succeed.
12. If you refuse to admit your mistakes, you can never be successful.
13. If you reject God and don't care, you are headed for trouble.
14. If you are wicked, you are as dangerous to the poor as a lion or bear attack.
15. Don't be stupid and oppress the people.
16. A murderer's conscience will drive him into hell. Don't stop him.
17. If you cheat, you will be destroyed.
18. Your playing around and not working bring poverty.
19. If you want to get rich quickly, you will quickly fail.
20. If you give preferred treatment to the rich, you are selling your soul for a piece of bread.
21. Trying to get rich quick is evil and will lead you into poverty.
22. If you rob your parents and say, "What's wrong with that?" you are no better than a murderer.

23. Your greed causes fighting.
24. Don't be a fool by trusting yourself.
25. A curse is upon you if you close your eyes to poverty.
26. Take heed: Good men go away when the wicked prosper.

CHAPTER 29

Things to Seek, Be, or Do

Chapter 29 brings to view a variety of things they should focus on and remember. Specifically, when good people are put in authority, the people rejoice. A just king gives stability to a nation. A king who is fair to the poor shall have a long reign. And if a tyrant is in charge, good men will live to see his downfall. It is wonderful for a nation to know and keep its laws. A wise son makes his father happy. Good men run from flattery and sing for joy. They care for others and know a poor man's rights. These wise men try to keep the peace. They hold their temper and try to cool down any situation. And the godly pray for those who want to kill them. God guides them, knowing the rich and poor depend on God for light. Sometimes mere words are not enough, and discipline is not enough. Scolding and spanking a child helps him learn. And if a son is disciplined, he will give his parents happiness and peace of mind. Humility brings honor. To trust in God means safety. The good hate the badness of the wicked. And if they want justice, they don't fawn all over the judge but ask the Lord for it.

Chapter 29
Key Points: Things to Seek, Be, or Do

1. When good people are in authority, you rejoice.
2. Be a wise son and make your father happy.
3. Encourage the king to be fair, and it will stabilize the nation.
4. Stay away from flattery and sing for joy.
5. Be good a good man and know the poor man's rights.
6. Be wise and try to keep the peace.
7. Be godly and pray for those who long to try to kill you.
8. Be wise and hold your temper in and play it cool.
9. Whether you are rich or poor, depend on God for light.
10. Encourage the king to be fair to the poor, and he will have a long reign.
11. If you scold and spank a child, you will help him learn.
12. Be the good men who stand up and watch the tyrant's downfall.
13. Discipline your son; he will give you happiness and peace of mind.
14. It's wonderful to encourage the nation to know and keep the laws.
15. Sometimes, your mere words are not enough; discipline is needed.
16. Your humility brings honor.
17. Your trust in God means safety.
18. If you want justice, don't fawn on the judge; ask the Lord for it.
19. If you are good, you will hate the badness of the wicked.

CHAPTER 29

What God Wants Us to Avoid

Chapter 29 shows us a variety of things to avoid. Specifically, when the wicked are in power, the people groan. The corrupt king takes bribes and destroys the nation. The wicked ruler will have wicked assistants on his staff. And when rulers are evil, their people are, too. Where there is ignorance of God, the people run wild. The man who refuses criticism will suddenly be broken and not get another chance. The son who hangs around prostitutes disgraces his father. Evil men are caught in the trap of flattery. The godless don't care about the poor. These hot-tempered fools start fights everywhere and get in all kinds of trouble. There is no arguing with him; they only rage and scoff. Tempers flare as the rebel shouts in anger. A child needs discipline. Left to his own devices, he brings shame to his mother and ignores wise words. His pride ends in a fall. Pamper a servant from childhood, and he will expect you to treat him as a son. The man who helps a thief hates himself. He knows the consequences and does it anyway. He turns from God and puts his trust in man, which is a dangerous trap. These wicked people hate the goodness of the good.

Chapter 29
Key Points: Things to Avoid

1. If you refuse criticism, you will suddenly be broken and not get another chance.
2. When the wicked are in power, the people groan.
3. Don't be like the son who hangs around prostitutes and disgraces his father.
4. Encourage others not to take bribes from the king, for it will destroy the nation.
5. Don't listen to flattery. It is a trap, and evil men are caught in it.
6. If you are godless, you don't care about the poor man's rights.
7. Don't be a fool who starts fights everywhere.
8. Don't argue with a fool; he only rages and scoffs, and tempers flare.
9. Don't be a rebel who shouts in anger.
10. Avoid the wicked assistants on the evil ruler's staff.
11. Don't have an undisciplined child who, left to himself, brings shame to his mother.
12. Take heed: If your leader is wicked, the people eventually become wicked.
13. When people are ignorant of God, they run wild.
14. Don't be like the rebel who ignores words of obedience and discipline and gets in trouble.
15. You will have more hope as a fool than as a man with a quick temper.
16. If you pamper a servant from childhood, he will expect you to treat him as a son.
17. Don't be hot-tempered or you'll start fights and get into all kinds of trouble.
18. Your pride ends in a fall.
19. If you help a thief, you will hate yourself. You know the consequences and do it anyway.
20. Have no fear of a man; that is a dangerous trap.
21. Don't be like the wicked who hate the goodness of the good.

CHAPTER 30

Things to Seek, Be, or Do

Chapter 30 includes messages from Agur, son of Jakeh, from Massa to Ithiel and Ucal. It illuminates the greatness of God, things that are both wonderful and hard to understand. Specifically, God goes back and forth between heaven and earth, holding the wind in his fists and the oceans in his cloak. Who created the world if anyone else but God? What is his name and his son's name, if you know it? Every word of God is true and proves all who come to him for protection are defended. Wise individuals will ask God to give them two favors before they die. First, they should ask for help never to tell a lie, and second, they should ask not to be provided either with poverty or riches. Instead, they should ask for just enough to meet their needs so they won't be rich and content without God or poor and tempted to steal.

Four things are too wonderful to understand:
1. The eagle gliding across the sky.
2. A serpent crawling on a rock.
3. A ship crossing a heaving ocean.
4. The growth of love between a man and woman.

Four things are small but unusually wise:
1. The ant who is not strong but saves food for the winter.
2. The delicate cliff badger who blends among the rocks to protect itself.
3. Locusts who have no leader but stay together.
4. The easy-to-catch and kill spider still found in the king's palace.

There are four stately monarchs:
1. The lion who is the king of animals and won't turn aside for anyone.
2. The peacock.
3. The he-goat.
4. A king as he leads his army.

Chapter 30
Key Points: Things to Seek, Be, or Do

1. Do you know who else but God goes back and forth between heaven and earth, holding the wind in his fists?
2. Do you know who else but God wraps the oceans in his cloak and creates the world?
3. If you know any other who has done it, what is his name and his son's name?
4. You know that every word of God proves true; he defends all who come to him for protection.
5. If you die, ask God for two favors: (1) help never to tell a lie, and (2) the gift of neither poverty nor riches, just enough to meet my needs.
6. Four things are too wonderful for you to understand:

   A. The eagle gliding across the sky.
   B. The serpent crawling on a rock.
   C. A ship crossing the heaving ocean.
   D. The growth of love between a man and a woman.

7. You should note four things that are unusually small but wise:

   A. The ant who is not strong but saves food for the winter.
   B. The cliff badger who, while delicate, protects itself by living among the rocks.
   C. The locusts who have no leaders but stay together in swarms.
   D. Spiders who are easy to catch and kill but are found in the king's palace.

8. You should recognize four stately monarchs:

   A. The lion, the king of animals, who won't turn aside for anyone.
   B. The peacock.
   C. The he-goat.
   D. A king as he leads his army.

CHAPTER 30

What God Wants Us to Avoid

Chapter 30 mentions various things to avoid in life. Specifically, mankind should know that they do not fully understand humanity, let alone God. Therefore, they should not add to God's words lest they are found to be liars and rebuked. No one should grow wealthy to the point that they may be content without God or so poor that they steal and insult God's name. They should never falsely accuse a man to his employer, or he will curse them for their sin. Despite their many sins, some feel faultless for cursing their father and mother. But the man who mocks his father and despises his mother will have his eye plucked out by ravens and eaten by vultures. Some are arrogant, disdainful, and proud beyond description, and they devour the poor with sharp knives.

There are four things that are never satisfied:
1. Hell.
2. A barren womb.
3. A barren desert.
4. Fire.

There are four things that make the earth tremble beyond understanding:
1. The slave who becomes king.
2. The rebel who prospers.
3. The bitter woman who finally marries.
4. The servant girl who replaces her mistress.

If someone is a proud fool and always plotting evil, he shouldn't brag but should use his hand to cover his mouth in shame. As the churning of cream yields butter and a blow to the nose causes bleeding, so does anger in causing quarrels.

Chapter 30
Key Points: Things to Avoid

1. You complain, "I am tired, God. I'm too stupid to be human; I cannot understand man, let alone God."

2. Do not add to God's words, lest he rebuke you and you are found to be a liar.

3. If you grow too rich, you may become content without God.

4. If you are poor, you may steal and insult God's name.

5. Never falsely accuse a man to his employer lest he curses you for your sin.

6. Don't be like those who curse their father and mother and feel faultless despite their many sins.

7. Don't be like those who are proud beyond description—arrogant, disdainful, and they devour the poor with sharp knives.

8. You should know there are four things that are never satisfied:

   A. Hell.
   B. Barren womb.
   C. Barren desert.
   I. Fire.

9. If you mock your father and despise your mother, you will have your eye plucked out by ravens and eaten by vultures.

10. Beware the prostitute who will sin and say, "What's wrong with that?"

11. You should note that there are four things that make the earth tremble:

   A. A slave who becomes king.
   B. A rebel who prospers.
   C. A bitter woman who finally marries.
   D. The servant girl who marries the mistress's husband.

12. You are a fool by plotting evil. So don't be proud and brag; cover your mouth with your hand in shame.

13. As the churning of cream creates butter and a blow to the nose causes bleeding, your anger causes quarrels.

CHAPTER 31

Things to Seek, Be, or Do

Chapter 31 comes from King Lemuel of Massa, taught at his mother's knee, and focuses on justice and the blessings of finding a good wife. Specifically, defend those who cannot help themselves. Speak up for the poor and needy so they can have justice. If you find a truly good wife, she is more precious than gems. Her husband trusts her, and she satisfies his needs. She will not hinder him but help him all his life. Her husband is well-known and sits in council chambers with civic leaders. She watches over her household and what goes on and is never lazy. She plans the day's work for the servant girls and is an energetic, hard worker. She watches for bargains and works far into the night. She inspects a field and buys it. She plants a vineyard with her own hands and buys imported foods from distant ports. She is up before dawn to cook breakfast for her family. She spins wool and flax. She has no fear of winter because she has made warm clothes for her family. She upholsters the finest tapestry, and her clothing is beautifully made from purple linen. She sews and gives generously to the poor and makes belted garments to be sold to merchants. She is a woman of strength and dignity and has no fear of old age. Her words are wise, and everything she says is full of kindness. Her children and husband stand and bless her. Her husband says, "There are many fine women in the world, but you are the best of all of them." It will be the woman who fears and has great reverence for God who shall be greatly praised. Praise her for the many fine things she does. Her good deeds will bring her honor and recognition from the nation's leaders.

Chapter 31
Key Points: Things to Seek, Be, or Do

1. Be like King Lemuel of Massa, who taught at his mother's knee.
2. Defend those who cannot help themselves.
3. Speak up for the poor and needy and see they get justice.
4. If you find a truly good wife, she is more than gems.
5. Be a husband who trusts his wife, and she will satisfy your needs.
6. Be a wife who does not hinder her husband but helps him all her life.
7. Be a wife who spins wool and flax.
8. Be a wife who buys imported foods from distant ports.
9. Be a wife who is up before dawn to cook breakfast for her family.
10. Be a wife who plans the day's work for servant girls.
11. Be a wife who inspects a field and buys it.
12. Be a wife who plants a vineyard with her own hands.
13. Be a wife who is an energetic hard worker.
14. Be a wife who watches for bargains and works far into the night.
15. Be a wife who sews for the poor and gives generously to the poor.
16. Be a wife who has no fear of winter because she makes warm clothes for her family.
17. Be a wife who upholsters the finest tapestry, and her own clothes are beautifully made of purple linen.
18. Be a wife whose well-known husband sits in the council chamber with civic leaders.
19. Be a wife who makes belted linen garments to be sold to merchants.
20. Be a woman of strength and dignity who has no fear of getting old.
21. As a wife, your words are wise, and kindness is the rule for everything you say.
22. Be a wife who watches over her household and what goes on and is never lazy.
23. Be a wife who has children who stand and bless her.

24. Be a husband who blesses his wife and says, "There are many fine women in the world, but you are the best of them all."
25. Be a woman who fears and has reverence for God, and you shall be greatly praised.
26. Be a woman who is praised for the many fine things she has done.
27. Your good deeds will bring you honor and recognition from the nation's leaders.

CHAPTER 31

What God Wants Us to Avoid

Chapter 31 ends the book of Proverbs with straightforward advice on women, alcohol, and beauty. Specifically, it contains a warning not to spend a lot of time wooing women, for it is the royal pathway to destruction. It's not for a king to drink wine and whisky. Otherwise, he will forget his duties and not give justice to the oppressed. Hard liquor is for those on their deathbed, and wine is for those with depression. People who drink are trying to forget their battles of misery and poverty. Some women forget God and focus on charm and beauty, which can be deceptive and fades with age.

Chapter 31
Key Points: Things to Avoid

1. Son, do not spend your time with women, the royal pathway to destruction.
2. Learn from this: Kings should not drink wine and whisky.
3. Avoid drinking, for even the king forgets his duties when this happens.
4. Avoid drinking, for like the king, you may forget to give justice to the oppressed.
5. You should use hard liquor for sick men on the brink of death and wine for deep depression.
6. Know that people drink to forget poverty and misery.
7. Your charm can be deceptive, and your beauty doesn't last.

SECTION TWO

LIVING PROVERBS PASSAGES

Categories of Things to Do

1. KEY POINTS FROM PROVERBS: BENEFITS OF THE POOR

1. They still have great wealth.
2. They are never kidnapped and held for ransom.
3. It is better to have little if they have reverence for God.
4. It is better to be poor and humble than the opposite.
5. The poor plan, but the rich throw insults.
6. It is better to be poor and honest than the opposite.
7. A poor man has no "friends."
8. The poor and rich are alike before the Lord.
9. Both the poor and rich depend on God for light.

2. KEY POINTS FROM PROVERBS: BUSINESS

1. The Lord demands fairness in every business deal.
2. Honest gain is better than dishonest wealth.
3. Many people beg the generous man; he has many "friends."
4. A business built by wise planning becomes strong through common sense and profits, using facts.
5. The wise man develops his business before he builds his home.
6. A faithful employee is as refreshing as a cool day in the hot summertime.
7. A wise man watches his business; riches disappear fast.
8. Watching one's business means having wool for clothing and goat's milk for food.

3. KEY POINTS FROM PROVERBS: WHAT CHARACTER IS AND WHAT IT PROVIDES

1. Truthfulness.
2. Kindness.
3. Humbleness.
4. Trust in God.
5. Ability to turn one's back on evil.
6. To be upright.
7. To do the right thing.
8. Ability to stay on the right path.
9. Ability to be good.
10. Ability to be part of God's family.
11. Nourishment for the soul.
12. Planning of good things.
13. Helps give joy.
14. Helps give self-control.
15. Helps one accept advice.
16. Helps one become wise.
17. Helps one think ahead.
18. Helps one become wiser by being with wise men.

4. KEY POINTS FROM PROVERBS: CHILDREN

1. Should obey their mother and father.
2. Should listen to the counsel of a mother and father for safety.
3. Should embrace a parent's instructions.
4. Should listen to parents to avoid prostitutes.
5. Should take advice to heart.
6. Should obey your father and write down his words.
7. Should believe a father's advice is a prized possession.
8. Should be level-headed, bringing happiness.
9. Should accept a father's rebuke.
10. Should consider each recommendation from his father.
11. Should be sensible in order to gladden his father.
12. Should believe his father is his glory.
13. As grandchildren, should be an older man's glory.
14. Should recognize the beautiful heritage of having an honest father.
15. Should have their character known by how they act, if that behavior is pure and right.
16. Should learn from parents to choose the right path and remain on it.
17. Should listen to a father's advice and an old mother's experience.
18. Should give pleasure to parents by being a wise son.
19. Should give his father joy by being a godly man.
20. Should make his father happy by being sensible.

5. KEY POINTS FROM PROVERBS: COMMUNICATION

1. One should speak the truth.
2. One should accept criticism in order to be on the road to the hall of fame.
3. One should accept that rebuke shows love.
4. One's bold reproof leads to peace.
5. The wise hold their tongue and show self-control.
6. Good counselors bring common sense.
7. One should talk less.
8. One should listen more.
9. One should give excellent and wise advice.
10. One should speak about what is helpful.
11. The wise are glad to be instructed.
12. The trusted person quiets all rumors.
13. There is safety in many counselors.
14. The meek become wise.
15. Honesty is its own defense.
16. Truth equals satisfaction.
17. Reliable communication is needed for progress.
18. Good advice refreshes.
19. One should stay cool when insulted.
20. The right words soothe and heal.
21. One should use words of encouragement.
22. One doesn't show off knowledge.
23. One should seek advice from friends.
24. Understanding is improved when one wants to be taught.
25. One should persuade with careful argument.
26. One should hate lies.
27. One should get all the advice possible and be wise.
28. One should use soft answers to turn away wrath.
29. Gentle words cause life and health.
30. Only the good can give good advice.

31. One should say the right thing at the right time.
32. One should accept constructive criticism.
33. Kind words delight the Lord.
34. Showing a smiling face reveals a glad heart.
35. A good man thinks before he speaks.
36. Understanding is better than silver.
37. Kind words are healthful and enjoyable, like honey.
38. Wise words express deep streams of thought.
39. Wise advice is like a good meal.
40. It pays to keep one's mouth shut.
41. The man of few words and a settled mind is wise.
42. Even the silent fool is thought to be wise.
43. Good advice lies deep within a counselor's heart.
44. One should keep their mouth shut and stay out of trouble.
45. One should listen to wise advice.
46. One should pass wise advice to others.
47. One should learn well by listening.
48. One should accept criticism and get all the help he can.
49. The Lord will rejoice over wise words and common sense.
50. There is safety in many counselors.
51. Don't go to war without counsel.
52. It's an honor to receive a frank reply.
53. Timely advice is as lovely as golden apples in a silver basket.
54. It's an honor to accept valid criticism.
55. Be patient; a soft tongue can break hard bones.
56. Good news is like cold water to the thirsty.
57. Tensions disappear when gossip disappears.
58. Open rebuke is better than hidden love.
59. Wounds from a friend are better than kisses from an enemy.
60. Friendly suggestions are pleasant as perfume.
61. Friendly discussions are as stimulating as iron striking iron.
62. People appreciate frankness over flattery.
63. Good men stay away from flattery and sing for joy.
64. One should ask God to keep him from ever telling a lie.

6. KEY POINTS FROM PROVERBS: CONFESSION

1. If a man confesses his mistakes, he gets another chance.

7. KEY POINTS FROM PROVERBS: COURAGE

1. Courage can sustain a broken body.

8. KEY POINTS FROM PROVERBS: DISCIPLINE/PUNISHMENT

1. Punishment is proof of love.
2. It helps to discipline children and keep them on the right path.
3. It helps to teach right from wrong.
4. Those corrected are on the pathway of life.
5. Those who accept a rebuke develop common sense.
6. One should punish the false witness and track him down.
7. One should discipline a son early while there is hope.
8. One should punish mockers and others will learn.
9. One should stamp out crime with severe punishment.
10. Punishment that hurts chases evil from the heart.
11. When the wicked meet disaster, good men return.
12. Punishment drives rebellion out of a youngster.
13. It keeps children out of hell.
14. If one corrects children with discipline, they won't die if a stick is used.
15. One should discipline a son, and he will give happiness and peace of mind.
16. Scolding and spanking a child helps him learn.
17. A wise son makes a father happy.
18. One should guide a horse with a whip, a donkey with a bridle, and a rebel with a rod to the back.
19. Sometimes, words are not enough; discipline is needed.

9. KEY POINTS FROM PROVERBS: YOUR ENEMY

1. If an enemy is hungry, one should give him food.
2. If an enemy is thirsty, one should give him a drink.
3. An undeserved curse has no effect and produces no harm, like a flying sparrow or swallow.
4. The good hate the badness of the wicked.

10. KEY POINTS FROM PROVERBS: FAMILY AND FRIENDS

1. A true friend is always loyal.
2. A brother is born to help in time of need.
3. Some friends are closer than brothers.
4. Wounds from a friend are better than kisses from the enemy.
5. One should never abandon a friend, either one's own or his father's.
6. A mirror reflects a man's face, but his chosen friends reveal his character.

14. KEY POINTS FROM PROVERBS: THE GODLY

1. The godly love to give.
2. Righteousness counts on judgment day.
3. The godly cause the city to prosper.
4. God delights in the good and those who try to be good.
5. Trust in God and find his favor.
6. The godly flourish like a tree.
7. The godly stand and defend.
8. They have real success.
9. They exalt the nation and have a refuge when they die.
10. God watches them.
11. Their road leads upwards, and they leave hell behind.
12. Their prayers are heard.
13. Their hearts gladden to God's knowledge.
14. Their prayers delight God.
15. Their white hair is their crown.
16. The Lord is the strong fortress that keeps them safe.
17. The path of the godly is safe and leads away from evil.
18. Happy men trust in God.
19. God blesses those who obey.
20. They learn by watching the ruin overtake the wicked.
21. The Lord preserves the upright.
22. Blessings shower those who rebuke sin.
23. They are as bold as lions.
24. When the godly are successful, everyone is happy.
25. Those who use God's wisdom are safe.
26. The godly pray for those who long to kill him.
27. When good people are in authority, the people rejoice.
28. Good men will live to see a tyrant's downfall.

15. KEY POINTS FROM PROVERBS: GOD'S GLORY

FOUR THINGS THAT ARE TOO WONDERFUL TO UNDERSTAND:

1. An eagle.
2. A serpent.
3. A ship heaving on the ocean.
4. Love between a man and a woman.

FOUR THINGS THAT ARE WISE:

1. The ant.
2. The cliff badger.
3. Locusts.
4. Spiders.

FOUR STATELY MONARCHS

1. The lion.
2. The peacock.
3. The he-goat.
4. The king as he leads his army.

16. KEY POINTS FROM PROVERBS: GOD REVEALED

1. God goes back and forth between heaven and earth.
2. Oceans are wrapped in God's cloak.
3. If anyone but God created the world, what is his name, and who is his son?
4. Every word of God proves true; he defends all who come to him for protection.

17. KEY POINTS FROM PROVERBS: HONORS

1. A wise man lets others praise him.
2. A man is tested by how he reacts to praise.
3. Humility brings honor.
4. It's an honor to receive a frank reply.

18. KEY POINTS FROM PROVERBS: HUMILITY

1. Humility ends in honor.
2. Humility brings honor.

19. KEY POINTS FROM PROVERBS: INCOME

1. The wise man gives the first part of his salary to God.
2. Earnings advance righteousness.
3. Income provides wealth from hard work.
4. The wise man asks God neither for poverty nor riches but for enough to meet his needs.

20. KEY POINTS FROM PROVERBS: JOY

1. A happy face means a glad heart.
2. A cheerful man means things are right.
3. A cheerful heart does good like a medicine.

21. KEY POINTS FROM PROVERBS: JUSTICE

1. The king can act as a judge.
2. The truthful witness never lies.
3. The truthful witness saves good men from death.
4. Hating bribes brings happiness.
5. Mercy and truth atone for injustice.
6. A bribe works like magic, and those who use them for good prosper.
7. A bribe does wonders; it brings men of importance in front of you.
8. The righteous finally win.
9. An honest witness is safe.
10. The wise man prepares for conflict, but victory comes from the Lord.
11. God is more pleased when people are just and fair than when they give him gifts.
12. The wise man gets the facts at any price and holds onto good sense.
13. The good love justice.
14. The good man rescues those unjustly sentenced to death.
15. He doesn't let the unjustly accused die.
16. He doesn't say that he didn't know if someone was unjustly accused.
17. God rewards according to individuals' deeds.
18. Like removing the dross from silver, corrupt men should be removed from the king's court, so his reign will be just and fair.
19. Those who follow the Lord care about justice.
20. Obeying the law is to fight evil.
21. Young men who obey the law are wise.
22. The man who wants to do the right thing gets a rich reward.
23. If someone wants justice, he shouldn't fawn on the judge but should ask the Lord for it.
24. It is wonderful for a nation to know and keep the laws.
25. The good man defends those who cannot help themselves.
26. He speaks up for the poor and the needy and sees that they get justice.

22. KEY POINTS FROM PROVERBS: THE KING

1. A growing population is the king's glory.
2. He rejoices in servants who know what to do.
3. He is helped by God to help judge people.
4. His right to rule depends on his fairness.
5. He rejoices when people are truthful and fair.
6. The wise man appeases the anger of the king.
7. Favors shine on those who try to please the king.
8. A king's approval is as refreshing as dew on the grass.
9. A king who acts as a judge weighs the evidence carefully—what is true and what is false.
10. The kingdom stands secure if the king is kind, honest, and fair.
11. The Lord directs the king's thoughts.
12. A king's friends are those who value grace and truth.
13. A king's privilege is to discover; God's privilege is to conceal.
14. Stability comes from honest and sensible leaders.
15. The king who hates dishonesty and bribes will have a long reign.
16. A king who is fair to the poor shall have a long reign.
17. A just king gives stability to the nation.

23. KEY POINTS FROM PROVERBS: LOVE

1. Love overlooks insults.
2. Love forgets mistakes.
3. God purifies hearts.
4. Kindness makes a man attractive.

24. KEY POINTS FROM PROVERBS: KEEP THE PEACE

1. It is better for a man to have soup with someone he likes than steak with someone he hates.
2. A dry crust eaten in peace is better than a steak eaten in strife.
3. A coin toss ends arguments.
4. It is better to live in an attic corner with a good woman than with a crabby woman in a lovely home.
5. It is better to live in a desert than with a quarrelsome woman.

25. KEY POINTS FROM PROVERBS: PHYSICAL GIFTS

1. If a man has good hearing and good eyesight, he should thank God who gave them to him.
2. The glory of young men is strength; for older men, their experience.

26. KEY POINTS FROM PROVERBS: PLANNING

1. Man makes plans, but God determines the outcome.
2. Man makes plans counting on God to help him.
3. Humans toss the coin; God controls the decision.
4. The Lord has made everything for his purpose.
5. The Lord directs our steps, so why try to understand what happens along the way?
6. A man's conscience is the Lord's searchlight exposing hidden motives.
7. A man should wait and see what plans God has for him.

27. KEY POINTS FROM PROVERBS: REVERENCE FOR GOD

1. Reverence for God adds life.
2. It adds hours to each day.
3. It brings blessings, the most incredible wealth.
4. It leads to life.
5. It helps dreams come true.
6. Success comes from obeying God.
7. Blessings will chase a person who reverences God.
8. The bond of the godly is goodwill.
9. Doing right honors God.
10. Reverence for God gives man deep strength.
11. It gives children refuge and security.
12. It is the fountain of life.
13. It keeps man from death.
14. It makes you wise and honored.
15. It helps you become truly good.
16. It pleases God and puts enemies at peace.
17. If a person keeps the commandments, he will keep his life.
18. Reverence for God gives life, happiness, and protection from harm.
19. A person should trust in the Lord. It was right in the past; it will be right in the future.
20. True humility and respect for the Lord lead to riches, honor, and long life.
21. A reverence for the Lord leads to a wonderful life.
22. Blessed is the man who reveres God.
23. Trusting God leads to prosperity.
24. Trusting God means reverence.

28. KEY POINTS FROM PROVERBS: SAVE OTHERS

1. A good man should win souls and be wise.

29. KEY POINTS FROM PROVERBS: SEX

1. A person should guard his affections.
2. He should avoid prostitutes.
3. It is better to have self-control than to control an army.
4. A good man should be faithful to his wife.
5. He should be faithful to the wife of his youth.
6. He should embrace his wife's love and charms.
7. Kindness makes a man attractive.

30. KEY POINTS FROM PROVERBS: TEACHING

1. A wise teacher makes learning a joy.
2. A pleasant teacher is the best teacher.
3. To learn, a person must want to be taught.

31. KEY POINTS FROM PROVERBS: TEMPER

1. A calm temper stops fights.
2. A wise man holds his temper.
3. It is better to be slow-tempered than famous.
4. It brings honor to a man to stay out of a fight.
5. Throw out the mocker and eliminate tension, fighting, and quarrels.
6. A wise man restrains anger and overlooks insults.

32. KEY POINTS FROM PROVERBS: A GOOD WIFE

1. A good wife is more precious than gems.
2. Her husband trusts her, and she satisfies his needs.
3. She will not hinder him but help him all his life.
4. Her husband is well-known and sits in council chambers with civic leaders.
5. She watches over her household and what goes on and is never lazy.
6. She plans the day's work for the servant girls.
7. She is an energetic, hard worker.
8. She watches for bargains and works far into the night.
9. She inspects a field and buys it.
10. She plants a vineyard with her own hands.
11. She buys imported foods from distant ports.
12. She is up before dawn to cook breakfast for her family.
13. She spins wool and flax.
14. She has no fear of winter because she has made warm clothes for her family.
15. She upholsters the finest tapestry, and her clothing is beautifully made from purple linen.
16. She sews and gives generously to the poor.
17. She makes belted garments to be sold to merchants.
18. She is a woman of strength and dignity and has no fear of old age.
19. Her words are wise, and everything she says is full of kindness.
20. Her children and husband stand and bless her.
21. Her husband says, "There are many fine women in the world, but you are the best of all of them."
22. It will be the woman who fears and has great reverence for God who shall be greatly praised.
23. Praise her for the many fine things she does.
24. Her good deeds will bring her honor and recognition from the nation's leaders.

33. KEY POINTS FROM PROVERBS: WHAT WISDOM IS AND WHAT IT PROVIDES

1. Wisdom brings insight.
2. It brings discernment.
3. It brings knowledge.
4. It brings understanding.
5. It brings peace.
6. It brings safety.
7. It helps you avoid traps.
8. It brings enjoyable life.
9. It helps you avoid evil people.
10. It helps you avoid prostitutes.
11. It helps you know right from wrong.
12. It helps guard your path.
13. It gives you long life.
14. It gives you riches.
15. It gives you pleasure.
16. It gives you great honors.
17. It is beloved like a sweetheart.
18. It is a beloved member of the family.
19. It is the fountain of life.
20. It is better than gold.
21. It is one of life's two great goals, along with common sense.
22. It is the tree of life.
23. It is right and true.
24. It gives understanding.
25. It gives common sense.
26. It hates lies, arrogance, corruption, and deceit.
27. It has no evil.
28. It is clear to everyone.
29. It loves all who love it.

30. It shows good judgment.
31. It helps you respect and fear God.
32. It gives riches, honor, justice, and righteousness.
33. It gives wealth.
34. It has been here before anything was created.
35. It will delight you.
36. It brings happiness.
37. It helps you become wiser.
38. It brings profit.
39. It comes easily to the man with common sense.
40. It is in the hearts of men with common sense.
41. It is the fountain of life.
42. It produces careful and persuasive speech.
43. It is the primary pursuit of the sensible.
44. Wisdom is mightier than strength.
45. He who loves wisdom loves his best interest and will be a success.
46. There is hope and a bright future when you enjoy wisdom.
47. It helps people stay on God's path.
48. Along with honey, it whets the appetite.

34. KEY POINTS FROM PROVERBS: THE WISE MAN

1. The wise man looks ahead.
2. His speech is respected.
3. He stays away from fools.
4. He is praised for his wisdom.
5. He is cautious and avoids danger.
6. He is patient and uses common sense.
7. He is crowned with knowledge.
8. He checks to see where he is going.
9. He plans well and receives mercy.
10. The wise man controls his temper, knowing anger causes mistakes.
11. He has a relaxed attitude that lengthens his life.
12. He is hungry for the truth.
13. He responds well to constructive criticism and is on the way to the wise man's hall of fame.
14. He stays on the right path.
15. He knows many counselors bring success.
16. He appeases the anger of the king.
17. He uses careful and persuasive speech.
18. He is open to new ideas and looks for them.
19. He restrains anger and overlooks insults.
20. If reproved, the wise man becomes wiser.
21. He draws out good advice from a counselor's heart.
22. He knows good sense is more valuable than jewels.
23. He saves for the future.
24. He conquers the strong levels of defense.
25. He learns by listening.
26. He sees difficulties ahead and plans for them.
27. He stays away from the treacherous road and saves his soul.
28. The wise man is mightier than the strong man.
29. The wise man watches for problems and prepares.
30. Men who encourage the upright are given a worthwhile award.
31. The wise man holds his temper and plays it cool.
32. A wise man tries to keep the peace.

35. KEY POINTS FROM PROVERBS: WORK

1. The good man works hard.
2. He works hard like the ant.
3. Working hard can help make one rich.
4. Working means not starving.
5. Work hard, make the most of the day while the sun shines.
6. Get your hands dirty and work.
7. Work leads to prosperity and blessings.
8. Work leads to becoming a leader.
9. Be diligent and make use of everything.
10. Work leads to plans developing and prospering.
11. The work of the godly will flourish.
12. Work brings profit.
13. Hunger is good if it makes someone work.
14. If work is committed to God, it will succeed.
15. A wise slave will rule a master's wicked sons.
16. Stay awake, work hard, and there will be plenty to eat.
17. Steady plodding brings prosperity.
18. Hardworking people are successful and will stand before kings.
19. The master may get better help from an untrained apprentice than a skilled rebel.
20. A worker should be able to eat from the food orchard he tends.
21. Hard work brings prosperity.

SECTION THREE

LIVING PROVERBS PASSAGES

Categories of Things to Avoid

1. KEY POINTS FROM PROVERBS (TO AVOID): ADULTERY

1. Avoid someone else's wife.
2. Adultery is like walking on coals.
3. It is like holding fire to the chest.
4. Those who commit adultery are utter fools; it destroys their soul.
5. Adultery angers a husband with jealousy. He will have no mercy, and there is no buying him off.

2. KEY POINTS FROM PROVERBS (TO AVOID): ALCOHOL

1. Wine gives false courage.
2. Liquor leads to brawls.
3. Fools let alcohol master them; it makes them stagger down the street.
4. Hard liquor is for sick men on the brink of death.
5. Wine is for deep depression.
6. People drink to forget poverty and misery.

3. KEY POINTS FROM PROVERBS (TO AVOID): CHARACTER FLAWS

1. One shouldn't be conceited.
2. The wise man doesn't resent correction.
3. People shouldn't fail to keep vital information to themselves.
4. Excessive sleep leads to poverty.
5. One shouldn't be hateful.
6. One shouldn't be prideful.
7. One shouldn't be arrogant.
8. One shouldn't be corrupt.
9. One shouldn't be full of deceit.
10. One shouldn't use poor judgment.
11. One shouldn't refuse to be corrected and lose his chance.
12. Pride ends in shame.
13. Cruelty destroys one's soul.
14. God hates stubbornness.
15. One shouldn't praise themselves.
16. One shouldn't brag about his plans.
17. Ambition and deceit are the same in that neither is satisfied.
18. A man who refuses to admit mistakes can never be successful.
19. Pride ends in a fall.
20. A man who helps a thief hates himself.
21. Some are proud beyond description: arrogant, disdainful, and devouring the poor.

4. KEY POINTS FROM PROVERBS (TO AVOID): CHILDREN

1. Sad is the mother of the rebel.
2. A fool despises a father's advice.
3. A rebellious son saddens his mother.
4. It is no fun to be a rebel's father.
5. A rebellious son is a grief to his father and a bitter blow to his mother.
6. A rebellious son is a calamity to his father.
7. A son mistreating his mother or father is a public disgrace.
8. A youngster's heart is full of rebellion.
9. God puts out the light of the man who curses his father or mother.
10. A son who belongs to a lawless gang shames his father.
11. A man who robs his parents is no better than a murderer.
12. An undisciplined child brings shame to his mother.
13. A man who mocks his father and despises his mother will have his eyes plucked by ravens and eaten by vultures.
14. Some curse their mother and father and feel faultless despite their many sins.

5. KEY POINTS FROM PROVERBS (TO AVOID): COMMUNICATION

1. The evil man is filled with curses and lies.
2. Hatred stirs quarrels.
3. Fools blurt out everything, leading to sorrow and trouble.
4. To hate is to be a liar.
5. Slander is equal to being a fool.
6. Talk too much and you'll say something inappropriate.
7. Words of a fool are plentiful but useless.
8. A liar's counsel and advice are shunned.
9. The wicked speak of rebellion.
10. Gossip spreads rumors.
11. Quarrelling with a neighbor is foolish.
12. Lies get a man in trouble.
13. Arguments come from pride.
14. Refusing criticism means poverty and disgrace.
15. The unreliable messenger halts progress.
16. The wicked man shames himself by lying.
17. A quick retort can't win.
18. A rebel has foolish talk that pricks his pride.
19. A simpleton believes what he is told.
20. A short-tempered man is a fool.
21. Hard words cause quarrels.
22. Complaining causes discouragement.
23. A rebel can't give good advice.
24. Mockers feed on the trash of lies.
25. Too few counselors mean things go wrong.
26. The evil man pours out evil words.
27. Reject criticism and harm yourself and your own interests.
28. A sad face means a broken heart.
29. Gossip separates the best of friends.
30. Idle lips are the devil's mouthpiece.

31. Liars enjoy liars.
32. Truth from a rebel is unexpected.
33. Lies from a king are unexpected.
34. A rebel doesn't care about facts; all he does is yell.
35. Rumors are dainty morsels eaten with great relish.
36. No one should go ahead with plans without the advice of others or go to war until all agree.
37. If someone loves to talk, he'll suffer the consequences; men die from saying the wrong thing.
38. Individuals must avoid being dishonest and rich.
39. A person should never be a liar or a false witness.
40. A person shouldn't tell his secrets to a gossip unless he wants it broadcast to the world.
41. Gossip is a dainty morsel eaten with great relish.
42. Pretty words hide a wicked heart, like the pretty glaze on a clay pot.
43. A man with hate in the heart may sound pleasant but he curses them in that same heart.
44. Flattery is a form of hatred and cruel wounds.
45. A man pretends to be kind, but his hatred will show for all to see.
46. The man who refuses criticism will suddenly be broken.

6. KEY POINTS FROM PROVERBS (TO AVOID): DEATH

1. The godless fear death.
2. The wide and pleasant road ends in death.
3. Despising the Lord's commandments ends in a man's death.

7. KEY POINTS FROM PROVERBS (TO AVOID): DISCIPLINE

1. Refusing reproof is stupid.
2. Refusing to discipline a son means the father doesn't love him.
3. The young mocker refuses a father's rebuke.
4. The Lord punishes those who stop being good.
5. God punishes those who rejoice over others' misfortunes.
6. A rebuke to a rebel is like 100 lashes to the back.
7. The son who has no discipline will ruin his life.

8. KEY POINTS FROM PROVERBS (TO AVOID): ENEMY

1. A man shouldn't rejoice when his enemy meets trouble, or the Lord may stop punishing the enemy and punish that man instead.

9. KEY POINTS FROM PROVERBS (TO AVOID): EVIL

1. Evil bows before the godly.
2. Those who plot evil get lost.
3. The Lord watches evil.
4. If someone repays evil for good, a curse is upon his head.
5. No one should repay evil with evil but should wait for the Lord to do it.
6. An evil man lives an evil life.
7. To plan evil is as wrong as doing it.
8. A curse is upon those who lead the godly astray.
9. A man becomes a fool by plotting evil. He shouldn't brag but should cover his mouth in shame.
10. If someone searches for evil, he will find God's curse.
11. The man with the warped mind is despised.
12. The kindness of godless men is cruel.
13. If a man is with evil men, he will become evil.

10. KEY POINTS FROM PROVERBS (TO AVOID): THE EVIL MAN

1. The evil man loves to eat.
2. He is the treacherous man who walks the rocky road.
3. He only wants to fight.
4. The bond of rebels is guilt.
5. The evil man sows strife.
6. He travels the wide and pleasant road that ends in death.
7. He is suspicious of everyone and tumbles into constant trouble.
8. God loathes the gifts of the lazy man, especially bribes.
9. An evil man is stubborn.
10. An evil man loves to harm others and has no chance to be a good neighbor.
11. A person shouldn't envy these evil men.
12. Evil men should leave the upright man alone and quit trying to cheat him out of his rights.
13. One calamity lays the evil man low.
14. The evil man has no future; his light will be snuffed out.
15. The man who sets traps for others will eventually be caught. The boulder will roll back on him.
16. A murderer's conscience will drive him into hell; no one should stop him.
17. Evil men are trapped by flattery.

11. KEY POINTS FROM PROVERBS (TO AVOID): EVIL MEN

1. Evil men are punished and find death.
2. They don't sleep until they die.
3. They make people stumble and fall.
4. They eat and drink violence.
5. They stumble in the dark.
6. A lack of common sense destroys them.
7. Their hopes are in vain.
8. They are undone by treachery.
9. When he dies, his hopes perish; they lived based on earthly life.
10. They get rich for a moment.

12. KEY POINTS FROM PROVERBS (TO AVOID): THE EVIL WOMAN

1. The evil woman lacks modesty.
2. She is sometimes a prostitute.
3. She corrodes a husband's strength.
4. She tears down everything.
5. She tears down her house.
6. A nagging wife annoys like dripping.
7. It's hard to live with a quarrelsome, complaining woman.
8. A cranky woman and dripping rain are the same things.
9. A person can't stop her complaints any more than he can stop the wind or hold onto something with oily hands.

13. KEY POINTS FROM PROVERBS (TO AVOID): FAMILY/ FRIENDS

1. It's harder to win back the friendship of an offended brother than capture a fortified city; the anger shuts people out like iron bars.
2. Some people are friends in name only.
3. Most people say what loyal friends they are, but are they telling the truth?
4. A man shouldn't visit his neighbor too often or he'll wear out his welcome.
5. Being happy-go-lucky around a broken heart is like stealing their jacket in cold weather.
6. A fool provokes a family to anger and resentment.
7. Nagging about mistakes parts the best of friends.
8. Not giving a promised gift is like the cloud in the desert that doesn't drop rain.
9. Pamper a servant, and he'll expect to be treated as a child.

14. KEY POINTS FROM PROVERBS (TO AVOID): FIGHTING/ QUARRELS

1. A quick-tempered man starts fights.
2. The fool would rather have steak with someone they hate than soup with someone they like.
3. A steak eaten in strife is worse than bread eaten in peace.
4. It's hard to stop quarrels once they start, so a person shouldn't let them begin.
5. Sinners love to fight.
6. The short-tempered man bears his own penalty; no one can help him.
7. Only fools insist on quarreling.
8. An angry man is silenced by giving him gifts.
9. It's far worse to live with a crabby woman in a lovely home than in an attic with a good man.
10. A person should avoid angry, short-tempered men or they will endanger that person's soul.
11. A harsh retort causes anger.
12. It is better to be in an attic with a good woman than in a beautiful home with a quarrelsome woman.
13. Shouting a pleasant greeting too early in the morning can be a curse.
14. Yanking a dog's ears is no more foolish than getting into someone else's business.
15. A quarrelsome man starts fights as quickly as a match lights paper on fire.
16. Jealousy is more dangerous and crueler than anger.
17. Greed causes fighting.
18. There is more hope for a fool than for a man with a quick temper.
19. The hot-tempered man starts fights and gets into all kinds of trouble.
20. A blow to the nose causes bleeding, and anger causes quarrels.

15. KEY POINTS FROM PROVERBS (TO AVOID): FOOLS

1. Fools refuse to be taught.
2. They exult in wrongdoing.
3. They don't trust themselves.
4. They don't trust their own wisdom.
5. They are promoted to shame.
6. They need to avoid foolishness.
7. Their fun is being bad.
8. He provokes his family to anger and resentment.
9. They will have nothing left.
10. They are servants to a wiser man.
11. They idle their time away.
12. They are quick-tempered and thinks he needs no advice.
13. They display foolishness.
14. They don't think ahead and brag about it.
15. They refuse to give up wrong plans.
16. They are short-tempered men.
17. They hate the patient.
18. Simpletons are crowned with folly.
19. They are despised for their folly.
20. Both hell and mankind are open to knowledge, but will they take it?
21. Their burden is their folly.
22. A man's foolishness ruins his chances, and he blames the Lord.
23. The man who strays from common sense ends up dead.
24. Fools plunge ahead with great confidence.
25. If a man enjoys folly, something is wrong.
26. It's safer to meet a bear robbed of her cubs than a man caught in his folly.
27. A fool's goals are at the end of the earth.
28. They get into constant fights; his mouth is his undoing, and his words endanger him.

29. It's not right for a fool to succeed or a slave to rule over a prince.

30. It is foolish and rash to make a promise to the Lord before counting the cost.

31. Honors go to fools like snow in the summer or rain in the harvest.

32. Arguing with a fool is foolish. Prick his conceit to prick his pride.

33. A proverb in the mouth of a fool is like a paralyzed leg.

34. A fool returns to folly like a dog to his vomit.

35. One thing worse than a fool is the conceited man.

36. The simpleton never looks ahead and suffers the consequences.

37. A man can crush a rebel into powder, but he can't stop the rebel from his foolishness.

38. A man is a fool to trust himself.

39. Fools start fights everywhere.

40. There is no arguing with a fool; his temper will flare.

16. KEY POINTS FROM PROVERBS (TO AVOID): GLUTTONY

1. Overeating honey makes you sick.
2. Overeating honey and thinking about the honors you deserve is harmful.
3. A man without self-control is as useless as the city's broken walls.
4. Even honey is tasteless to the full man.

17. KEY POINTS FROM PROVERBS (TO AVOID): GOD HATES

1. God hates haughtiness.
2. God hates murderers.
3. God hates those who plot evil.
4. He hates those eager to do wrong.
5. He hates the false witness.
6. He hates those sowing discord.
7. He hates those who don't keep promises.
8. The Lord despises those who say bad is good and good is bad.
9. No one should add to God's words, lest he rebukes him to be a liar.
10. Man complains, "I am tired God; I cannot understand man, let alone God."

18. KEY POINTS FROM PROVERBS (TO AVOID): JUSTICE

1. Cheaters will be destroyed.
2. It's wrong for a judge to favor the wicked and condemn the innocent.
3. How stupid and a shame to decide before knowing the facts.
4. Any story sounds true until the other side is told and straightens the record.
5. A false story from a witness shall be punished, and a liar caught.
6. A worthless witness cares nothing for the truth; he enjoys sinning too much.
7. The Lord despises every kind of cheating.
8. The Lord loathes all cheating and dishonesty.
9. Justice is a calamity to evildoers.
10. People justify every deed, but God directs their motives.
11. No one should move the ancient boundaries; that is stealing.
12. A man shouldn't testify against an innocent neighbor.
13. A man shouldn't pay someone back for meanness.
14. It is wrong to sentence the poor and let the rich go free.
15. A man must not be a hothead or rush to court, or it could mean shameful defeat.
16. A man should keep information to himself, or he could be accused of slander.
17. Evil men don't understand the importance of justice.
18. God doesn't listen to the prayers of those who flout the law.
19. A fool refuses the facts.
20. A false witness always lies.
21. A false witness is a traitor.
22. It is wrong to accept a bribe to twist justice.
23. It is shortsighted to fine godly men for being good or punishing nobles for being honest.
24. A false witness must be punished.

19. KEY POINTS FROM PROVERBS (TO AVOID): THE KING

1. A dwindling nation is the king's doom.
2. A king is angry with servants who cause trouble.
3. Anger of the king is the messenger of death.
4. It is horrible for the king to do evil.
5. The king's anger is as dangerous as the lion's.
6. The king's anger is like a roaring lion. Rouse him and risk your life.
7. The unjust tyrant will reap disaster, and his reign of terror will end.
8. No one can comprehend the height of heaven, size of the earth, or what goes on in a king's mind.
9. No one should demand an audience with the king, or he could be disgraced.
10. Only a stupid person oppresses his people.
11. Moral rot within the nation means the government topples easily.
12. The king who demands bribes destroys the nation.
13. Kings should not drink wine or whisky.
14. A king's drinking will make them forget their duties or give justice to the oppressed.

20. KEY POINTS FROM PROVERBS (TO AVOID): THE LAZY MAN

1. Putting confidence in an unreliable man is like chewing with a sore tooth or running on a broken foot.
2. The lazy man sticks to his bed like a door to its hinges.
3. A lazy man can't lift food to his mouth.
4. The lazy man claims he is wiser than seven wise men.

21. KEY POINTS FROM PROVERBS (TO AVOID): LYING

1. A man should avoid turning from the truth.
2. He should avoid lies and deception.
3. He will be destroyed over dishonesty.
4. God hates cheating.
5. The false man is known for lies, deceit, and cutting remarks.
6. Plotting evil and lies are exposed.
7. Telling lies is like wounding someone with an axe or arrow.
8. The man caught lying and saying he is "fooling" is like the mad man throwing arrows and firebrands.
9. A man should never falsely accuse another to his employer, lest he be cursed.

22. KEY POINTS FROM PROVERBS (TO AVOID): MOCKER/ SCORNER

1. The mocker/scorner ends in trouble.
2. He brings terror.
3. He brings anguish.
4. He brings distress.
5. He eats bitter fruit.
6. He ends in death.
7. He is the evil man.
8. Mockers will be mocked.
9. A man should avoid the mocker who hates him for helping.
10. If someone despises God's words, he will find trouble.
11. Sin means to despise God.
12. Mockers never find wisdom.
13. Rebel against God and die.
14. The mocker stays away from wise men because they hate to be scolded.
15. The mocker feeds on lies.
16. Where there is ignorance of God, people run wild.
17. The mocker is the scourge of mankind.
18. No one can stand against the Lord.
19. Mockers are proud, haughty, and arrogant.
20. Mockers and rebels will be severely punished.
21. Humans think they are right, but is God convinced?
22. A man proposes, but God disposes.
23. The man who rejects God is headed for trouble.

23. KEY POINTS FROM PROVERBS (TO AVOID): MONEY

1. Most will be less happy with money than common sense.
2. Don't be someone who doesn't pay their debts
3. A man shouldn't guarantee the debts of others.
4. Ill-gotten gain leads to short happiness.
5. Lazy men are poor.
6. The wicked man's riches will stop.
7. The evil man curses his own luck.
8. The self-sufficient fall on their faces.
9. Wealth is the only strength of the rich man.
10. The evil man squanders money on sin.
11. Riches won't matter.
12. Mere money is the only honor of the cruel man.
13. A man should avoid vouching for the credit of a stranger.
14. The evil man is rich for a moment.
15. If a man holds tight, he will lose everything.
16. Anyone who trusts his money will go down.
17. Dishonest money brings grief to the family.
18. The rich man thinks his wealth is now an impregnable wall of defense. What a dreamer!
19. The rich man answers with insults.
20. A man should avoid being both dishonest and rich.
21. A wealthy man has many "friends."
22. A poor man's brothers turn from him in embarrassment; how much more his friends.
23. It is better to be poor than to be dishonest.
24. "Utterly worthless," says the buyer, haggling over the price but then brags about their bargain.
25. It is risky to make a loan to a stranger.
26. Cakes bought by ill-gotten gain will turn into gravel in a man's mouth.
27. A fortune can be made from cheating, but a curse goes with it.

28. The foolish man spends whatever he gets.
29. Dishonest gain will never last.
30. Hasty speculation brings poverty.
31. The simpleton prefers riches, silver, and gold over a good name.
32. As the rich rule the poor, so the borrower is a servant to the lender.
33. Those who gain by robbing the poor or bribing the rich end in poverty.
34. Unless a man has extra cash, he shouldn't countersign the note.
35. The world's poorest credit risk is one who pays a stranger's debt.
36. Money from exploiting the poor will be given to those who pity them.
37. It's worse to cheat and be rich than the opposite.
38. The man who wants to get rich quickly will quickly fail.
39. Giving preferred treatment to the rich is selling one's soul for a piece of bread.
40. Get rich quick schemes are evil and lead to poverty.
41. Rich men are arrogant. Their real "poverty" is evident to the poor.
42. If a man grows too rich, he may not be content with God.

24. KEY POINTS FROM PROVERBS (TO AVOID): WRONG PATH

1. The wrong path will make a man limp and stumble along the way.
2. It takes sidetracks instead of the right path.
3. It fails to keep feet from danger.
4. The rebel walks a thorny, treacherous road.
5. When a man is gloomy, everything seems to go wrong.

25. KEY POINTS FROM PROVERBS (TO AVOID): THE POOR

1. Anyone who oppresses the poor insults God.
2. Mocking the poor is mocking God.
3. Shut your ears to the cries of the poor, and you'll be ignored during your own time of need.
4. No one should rob the poor and sick; the Lord is their defender and will punish him.
5. A curse is upon those who close their eyes to poverty.
6. When a poor man oppresses a poorer person, it's like a flood sweeping away their last hope.
7. The godless don't care about the poor man's rights.
8. If a man is poor, he may steal and insult God.

26. KEY POINTS FROM PROVERBS (TO AVOID): PRIDE

1. Pride disgusts the Lord.
2. The proud shall be punished.
3. Pride goes before the fall.
4. Haughtiness goes before the fall.
5. Boasting is looking for trouble.
6. Pride ends in destruction.

27. KEY POINTS FROM PROVERBS (TO AVOID): PROSTITUTES

1. A man should avoid the lips and flattery of the prostitute.
2. Her house is the house of death.
3. Men who visit her are destroyed.
4. The prostitute's house equals death and hell.
5. A man should avoid the crooked trail to her house, her kiss, and the corner street where she hangs out.
6. Embracing her leads to a cruel and merciless life.
7. Being with a prostitute leads to a loss of honor and wealth.
8. Anyone who embraces her becomes a slave to foreigners.
9. The prostitute equals shame, anguish, and syphilis.
10. Being with her ends in public disgrace and regret.
11. Being with her means being held by sin and being doomed.
12. She leads to poverty and costs a man his life.
13. A man must avoid her seduction and temptation.
14. He must avoid her seductive dress.
15. He must avoid her perfumed sheets.
16. He must avoid her seductive speech and flattery.
17. He avoids her promises of pleasure and that she is alone.
18. Falling to a prostitute is like being chopped at the butcher, a deer taking an arrow, or being a bird caught in a trap.
19. No one should think of her or where she walks.
20. Her house is the road to hell.
21. A man must avoid her loud brashness; she is full of shame and lust.
22. He must avoid her promise of stolen melons and apples.
23. Her customers are citizens of hell.
24. A prostitute is a dangerous trap; those cursed are caught in it.
25. Prostitutes are a deep and narrow grave.
26. Prostitutes wait for their victims.
27. Men unfaithful to their wives are caught in this sin.
28. A son who hangs around prostitutes disgraces his father.

29. How can a prostitute sin and say, "What's wrong with that?"
30. A man shouldn't spend time with women; it is the royal path to destruction.
31. Charm can be deceptive, and beauty doesn't last.

28. KEY POINTS FROM PROVERBS (TO AVOID): THE REBEL

1. The rebel rushes into war without counsel.
2. The rebel's schemes are sinful.
3. A man should avoid associating with radicals; it ends in sudden disaster.
4. The rebel misusing an illustration to make a point is no more felt than the thorn in the hand of the drunkard.
5. Honoring a rebel will backfire like a stone in a slingshot.
6. Trusting a rebel with a message is like drinking poison or cutting off one's feet.
7. The rebel always needs a rod to his back.
8. A rebel's frustrations are heavier than sand and rocks.
9. The man who strays from home is like a bird away from its nest.
10. A rebel ignores words of obedience and discipline and gets in trouble.
11. A rebel shouts in anger.

29. KEY POINTS FROM PROVERBS (TO AVOID): SELFISHNESS

1. People curse other people over price.
2. The selfish man quarrels, breaks the code of conduct, and demands his way.

30. KEY POINTS FROM PROVERBS (TO AVOID): SIN

1. Sin leads to sorrow.
2. The sinner's road is dark and gloomy.
3. Curses chase sinners.
4. When sinners die, their wealth goes to the godly.
5. Sin brings disgrace.
6. It is dangerous and sinful to rush into the unknown.
7. Who can stand before God and say, "I am sinless."
8. Pride, lust, and evil actions are all sins.

31. KEY POINTS FROM PROVERBS (TO AVOID): SPIRIT

1. A broken spirit makes one sick.
2. When courage dies, what hope is left?
3. A man is a poor specimen if he can't take the pressure of adversity.

32. KEY POINTS FROM PROVERBS (TO AVOID): TEACHING

1. A rebellious teacher spouts foolishness.
2. It is senseless to pay tuition to educate a rebel with no heart for the truth.
3. A man should stop listening to the teaching that contradicts what he knows.
4. The simpleton learns by seeing scorners punished.
5. The rebel despises wisdom and won't be chosen as a counselor.

33. KEY POINTS FROM PROVERBS (TO AVOID): THEFT

1. The crook will slip and fall.
2. Crooks are jealous of each other's loot.
3. A thief who steals for hunger can be forgiven if he repays seven times.

34. KEY POINTS FROM PROVERBS (TO AVOID): THE WICKED

1. The wicked are cursed.
2. They should be avoided.
3. They have hearts full of rebellion.
4. They stir discontent.
5. The names of wicked men will stink.
6. The wicked man's fears come true.
7. Disaster strikes and they are whirled away.
8. They lack reverence for God, so they can't expect a long life.
9. God destroys them.
10. They fall below their load of sins.
11. They are only rewarded on earth.
12. They fall into danger.
13. Their evil words destroy.
14. They are filled with moral decay.
15. They drive the city downhill.
16. The godless man's death is celebrated.
17. They can expect wrath.
18. They are condemned by God.
19. They will have no success.
20. They accuse and perish.
21. They have constant trouble.
22. The wicked love company and lead others into sin.
23. The wicked are made for punishment.
24. The wicked stare into space, planning evil deeds.
25. The wicked enjoy fellowship with the wicked.
26. They plunge ahead and fall.
27. Their anxious hearts are heavy.
28. Their sins crush them at death.
29. Their jealousy rots their lives.
30. The Lord hates their gifts.
31. The Lord despises their deeds.

32. The Lord is far from the wicked.
33. The Lord hates the thoughts of the wicked.
34. They live for rebellion and will be severely punished.
35. The wicked will finally lose.
36. The wicked are unfair; their violence boomerangs and destroys them.
37. The Lord ruins the plans of the wicked.
38. No one should envy the wicked or covet their riches.
39. If someone calls the wicked "innocent," he'll be cursed by nations.
40. Compromising with the wicked is like polluting a fountain or spring.
41. The wicked flee when no one is watching them.
42. A wicked man is dangerous to the poor.
43. When the wicked prosper, good men go away.
44. The wicked hate the goodness of the good.
45. When rulers are wicked, so are the people.
46. A wicked ruler will have wicked assistants on staff.
47. When the wicked are in power, people groan.
48. When the wicked succeed, everyone is sad.

35. KEY POINTS FROM PROVERBS (TO AVOID): IGNORING WISDOM

1. If a man refuses wisdom, he'll be injured.
2. If a man refuses wisdom, he loves death.
3. If a man scorns wisdom, he hurts himself.
4. Those with no common sense are beaten as a servant.
5. Without wise leadership, the nation is in trouble.
6. Hope deferred makes a heart sick.
7. Laughter can't hide a heavy heart.
8. Wisdom must be shouted before a fool will hear it.
9. Strength is weaker than wisdom.
10. A strong man is weaker than a wise man.

36. KEY POINTS FROM PROVERBS (TO AVOID): WORK

1. Lazy men are poor.
2. The lazy man is a pain to his employer.
3. Fools are too proud to work and starve.
4. Be lazy and never succeed.
5. Lazy hunters won't prepare what they catch.
6. The poor man has good soil but is robbed by injustice.
7. Lazy people want things but get little.
8. The stable is clean, but there is no income.
9. Work for the wicked will perish.
10. Talk brings poverty.
11. A lazy fellow has had trouble his whole life.
12. Idle hands are the devil's workshop.
13. The lazy man is the brother of the saboteur.
14. The lazy man sleeps and goes hungry.
15. Some men are so lazy they won't feed themselves.
16. If a man won't plow in the cold, he won't eat in the harvest.
17. If a man loves sleep, he will live in poverty.
18. The lazy man longs for things but refuses to work.
19. A man who loves pleasure, wine, and luxury ends in poverty.
20. The simpleton does not plan and suffers the consequences.
21. The lazy man is full of excuses: "I can't work, I might meet a lion."
22. A man shouldn't carouse with drunkards and gluttons; they are on their way to poverty.
23. Too much sleep clothes a man in rags.
24. The lazy man's field has thorns, weeds, and broken walls.
25. Extra sleep, slumber, and folding hands to rest lead to poverty.
26. The lazy man won't work because of a lion.
27. Playing around and not working brings poverty.

37. KEY POINTS FROM PROVERBS (TO AVOID): VIOLENT MEN

1. Violent men rob.
2. They kill.
3. They murder.
4. They end in violent death.
5. They demand their own way.
6. They follow the evil path.
7. They have needless fights.
8. Their violence is an abomination.
9. No one should envy godless men or their company; they spend their day plotting violence and evil.

38. KEY POINTS NEVER SATISFIED AND MAKES THE EARTH TREMBLE

Four Things That Are Never Satisfied:

1. Hell.
2. A barren womb.
3. A barren desert.
4. Fire.

Four Things That Make the Earth Tremble:

1. A slave who becomes a king.
2. A rebel who prospers.
3. A bitter woman who finally marries.
4. The servant girl who marries the mistress's husband.

.

SECTION FOUR

LIVING PROVERBS PASSAGES

The Characteristic Traits of Proverbs

List of General Proverbs Personal Profile Traits

1. Whether poor or rich, they depend on God.
2. They use fairness in business.
3. They are honest.
4. They are wise planners.
5. They build their business before home.
6. They are faithful employees.
7. They are truthful.
8. They are kind.
9. They are humble.
10. They try to do the right thing.
11. They have joy.
12. They have self-control.
13. They listen and accept advice.
14. They think ahead.
15. They always trust in God.
16. They are wise.
17. They obey their mother and father.
18. They accept discipline.
19. They are sensible.
20. They avoid prostitutes.
21. They bring good news.

22. They share kind and wise words.
23. They are men of few words.
24. They give good advice.
25. They are patient.
26. They speak the truth.
27. They hold their tongue.
28. They consult with wise counselors.
29. They listen more.
30. They talk less.
31. They speak what is helpful.
32. They quiet rumors.
33. Their honesty is its own defense.
34. They stay calm.
35. They are slow to anger.
36. They seek advice from friends.
37. They persuade with careful argument.
38. They hate lies.
39. They use kind words.
40. They think before speaking.
41. They use gentle and soft words to turn away wrath.
42. They avoid gossip.
43. They confess their mistakes.
44. They have courage.
45. They discipline their children.
46. They teach right from wrong.
47. They punish false witnesses.
48. They punish mockers.
49. They stamp out crime.
50. They drive rebellion out of youngsters.
51. They give food and drink to enemies.
52. They are a true friends.
53. They are a true brothers.
54. They love to give to others.

55. They get rich by giving.
56. They help the poor.
57. They honor God.
58. They are the generous man.
59. They protect the poor man's rights.
60. They are a strong anchor.
61. They are on firm footing.
62. They are guided by honesty.
63. They give life-giving fruit.
64. They have common sense.
65. They are concerned for animals.
66. They are known for speaking the truth.
67. Their life is full of light.
68. They are protected from harm.
69. They think before speaking.
70. They eat to live and avoid gluttony.
71. They leave an inheritance for their children.
72. They love justice.
73. They live a godly life.
74. They rise after being tripped.
75. They stand their ground and defend it.
76. Their prayers are heard.
77. Their prayers delight God.
78. They are happy and happily trust in God.
79. They are blessed by rebuking sin.
80. They are bold like a lion.
81. They are good leaders.
82. They use God's wisdom.
83. They pray for those who wish them harm.
84. They are humble when praised.
85. Their humility brings honor.
86. The first part of their salary goes to God.

87. Their earnings are used to advance righteousness.
88. They ask for enough to meet their needs.
89. They have a cheerful heart.
90. They are a truthful witness.
91. They show mercy.
92. They are just and fair.
93. They get the facts before deciding.
94. They love justice.
95. They rescue the unjustly accused.
96. They are rewarded for their deeds.
97. They obey the law.
98. They ask the Lord for justice.
99. They defend the helpless.
100. They speak for the poor and needy.
101. Their love overlooks insults and forgets mistakes.
102. They keep the peace.
103. They let the Lord direct their steps.
104. They have reverence for God.
105. They obey God.
106. They try to do the right thing.
107. They try to please God.
108. They keep the commandments.
109. They win souls.
110. They guard affections.
111. They are true to their wives.
112. They embrace their wives' love and charms.
113. They avoid prostitutes.
114. They are wise teachers.
115. They make learning a joy.
116. They are open to teaching.
117. They hold their temper.
118. They stay out of fights.
119. They get rid of tension by throwing out a mocker.

120. They seek wisdom.
121. They know wisdom has many benefits:

    A. Wisdom provides insight.
    B. Wisdom gives peace.
    C. Wisdom enriches life.
    D. Wisdom avoids evil.
    E. Wisdom is the fountain of life and tree of life.

122. They know wisdom is helping them in all facets of life.
123. They work hard to provide for their needs.

SECTION FIVE

LIVING PROVERBS PASSAGES

The Organized Ideal Proverbial Profile

Organized Proverbs
Personal Profile

Business

1. Proverbs individuals use fairness in business.
2. They think ahead.
3. They are wise planners.
4. They build their business before their home.
5. They are faithful employees.
6. They seek advice from their friends.
7. They consult wise counselors.
8. They are good leaders.
9. They work hard to provide for their needs.

Character

1. Proverbs individuals are kind.
2. They are humble.
3. They are humble when praised.
4. They are joyful.
5. They do the right thing.

6. They are wise.
7. They are sensible.
8. They have common sense.
9. They are patient.
10. They are courageous.
11. They confess their mistakes.
12. They are guided by honesty.
13. They are on a firm footing.
14. They have a strong anchor.
15. They love justice.
16. They rise after being tripped.
17. They stand up and defend others.
18. They are happy.
19. They have a cheerful heart.
20. They are bold like a lion.

Communication

1. Proverbs individuals are honest, which is its own defense.
2. They are truthful.
3. They accept advice.
4. They listen more.
5. They talk less.
6. They think before speaking.
7. They quiet rumors.
8. They avoid gossip.
9. They hold their tongue.
10. They give good advice.
11. They share kind words.
12. They share the good news.
13. They are men of few words.

14. They speak what is helpful.
15. They speak the truth.
16. They hate lies.
17. They persuade with careful argument.

Demeanor

1. Proverbs individuals have self-control.
2. They stay calm.
3. They are slow to anger.
4. They use gentle words to turn away wrath.
5. They hold their temper as much as possible.
6. They stay out of fights.

Discipline

1. Proverbs individuals accept discipline.
2. They obey their mother and father.
3. They eat to live and avoid gluttony.

Generosity

1. Proverbs individuals love to give.
2. They get rich by giving.
3. They help the poor.
4. They are generous people overall.
5. They are concerned for the welfare of animals.
6. They leave an inheritance for their children.

Forgiveness

1. Proverbs individuals give food and drink to the enemy.
2. They show mercy.
3. They pray for those who wish him harm.
4. They overlook insults.
5. They forget mistakes.

Justice

1. Proverbs individuals love justice.
2. They obey the law.
3. They are a truthful witness.
4. They are just and fair.
5. They get the facts.
6. They rescue the unjustly accused.
7. They defend the helpless.
8. They speak for the poor and needy.
9. They keep the peace.
10. They ask the Lord for justice.
11. They get rid of tension by throwing out mockers.

Loyalty

1. Proverbs individuals are true friends.
2. They are true brothers.

Parenting

1. Proverbs individuals discipline their children.
2. They teach their children right from wrong.
3. They drive rebellion out of youngsters.

Sex

1. Proverbs individuals guard their affections.
2. They avoid prostitutes.
3. They are men who are faithful and true to their wives.
4. They embrace their wives' love and charms.

Teaching

1. Proverbs individuals are wise teachers.
2. They are open to other teachings.
3. They make learning a joy.

Wisdom

1. Proverbs individuals use wisdom for more insight.
2. They use wisdom to achieve peace.
3. They use wisdom to enrich life.
4. They use wisdom to avoid evil.
5. They understand wisdom is the fountain of life.
6. They understand wisdom is the tree of life.

Worshiping God

1. Proverbs individuals have reverence for God.
2. They obey God.
3. They honor God.
4. They always try to please God.
5. They bear life-giving fruit.
6. They have a life full of light.
7. They have reverence for God, which keeps them from harm.
8. They live a godly life.
9. Whether poor or rich, they depend on God.
10. They happily trust in God.
11. They know their prayers are heard.
12. They know that God delights in their prayers.
13. God blesses them because he rebukes their sins.
14. They use God's wisdom.
15. Their humility brings honor.
16. They give the first part of their salary to God.
17. They use their earnings to advance righteousness.
18. They ask God for enough to meet their needs.
19. They let the Lord direct their steps.
20. They are rewarded for their deeds.
21. They try to keep the commandments.
22. They win souls for God.
23. They seek God's wisdom.

SECTION SIX

LIVING
PROVERBS PASSAGES

The Final Composite Proverbs Profile

The Final Composite Proverbs Profile

BUSINESS/EMPLOYMENT: Proverbs individuals are hardworking and faithful employees, using fairness in all business dealings. They plan ahead, seek advice, and build their employment and business before making a home.

CHARACTER: Proverbs individuals are happy, joyful, honest, wise, kind, and humble. God's followers are patient and have common sense. They admit their mistakes, defend others, are courageous in their beliefs, and can rise after falling.

COMMUNICATION: Proverbs individuals listen more and talk less. True followers are honest. They hold their tongue and try to avoid rumors and gossip. They share what is helpful and kind and bring good news and good advice.

DEMEANOR: Proverbs individuals have self-control, stay calm, and are slow to anger.

DISCIPLINE: Proverbs individuals accept discipline and obey their parents. They also are disciplined in their lives and eat to live as opposed to living to eat.

GENEROSITY: Proverbs individuals love to give, are generous when helping the poor, and are concerned about the welfare of animals. Parents leave an inheritance for their children.

FORGIVENESS: Proverbs individuals overlook insults, show mercy, pray for those who wish them harm, and even give food and drink to their enemies.

JUSTICE: Proverbs individuals obey the law and speak the truth. They are honest witnesses. They rescue the unjustly accused and defend the helpless and poor. They strive to keep the peace. They reduce tension by throwing out the mocker.

LOYALTY: Proverbs individuals are true friends and true brothers.

PARENTING: Proverbs individuals drive rebellion out of their children with discipline and teach them right from wrong.

SEX: Proverbs individuals guard their affections, remain faithful to their spouses, and avoid prostitutes.

TEACHING: Proverbs individuals use wisdom to teach. They teach with joy and are open to new learning.

WISDOM: Proverbs individuals embrace wisdom, knowing it is the tree of life that enriches, gives insight, and promotes peace while helping them avoid evil.

WORSHIPING GOD: Proverbs individuals revere God, knowing his life-giving fruit and light blesses them and keeps them from harm. They know God directs their steps, answers their prayers, meets their needs, helps them rebuke sin, and win souls, so they are rewarded for their faithfulness.

About the Author

Kevin M. Thomas is an award-winning author with titles such as *Tao Te Ching De-Coded*, *Why Daughters Need Their Dads*, *Wisdom and Virtue*, *The Great Path*, *Chinese Spiritual Thoughts*, and *The Happiest Women*. He has a varied background in medicine, alternative health, counseling, religion, and mind—body healing. He is an ordained deacon minister. Kevin is passionate about promoting and delivering positive change to any person, and he strives to effect personal growth in individuals via mind—body—spirit research and application. Finally, he considers his relationship with God and his unconditional love for his children—Isiah, Caroline, Kimberly, and Cheyenne—his greatest treasures.

Book Summary

The Bible's book of Proverbs is filled with short sayings provided for life and moral and spiritual instruction. Seeking this wisdom helps one gain a happier life while helping to avoid pitfalls that can pop up. In this book, *Living the Life of Proverbs,* all thirty-one chapters are summarized and collated into groups for easy understanding. Multiple translations from the NIV to the NLT and more texts were explored to help give this book a solid foundation for discovery. In addition, over 120 characteristic traits of the ideal person are put into fourteen categories to help further people's understanding of the areas in their lives needing work to please God and become a better Christian.

KETNA PUBLISHING: Kevin Thomas and Erik Naugle make up KETNA Publishing, a small hometown publisher in mid-Michigan. Their goal is to deliver high-quality information into the hands of the people so they can positively change their lives via body, mind, and spirit application. You can contact KETNA Publishing at grobthom@aol.com or write to KETNA Publishing, P.O. Box 90861, Burton, Michigan, 48509.